ENGLISH
COMMON CORE
EDITION

Published by
TOPICAL REVIEW BOOK COMPANY
P. O. Box 328
Onsted, MI. 49265-0328
E-mail: sales@topicalrbc.com • Website: topicalrbc.com

ENGLISH

Aug 2017

COMMON CORE EDITION

TABLE OF CONTENTS

Published by
TOPICAL REVIEW BOOK COMPANY
P. O. Box 328
Onsted, MI. 49265-0328
E-mail: sales@topicalrbc.com • Website: topicalrbc.com

Part 1
Multiple-Choice Questions

Directions (1–24): Closely read each of the three passages below. After each passage, there are several multiple choice questions. Select the best suggested answer to each question and record your answer in the space provided. You may use the margins to take notes as you read.

Reading Comprehension Passage A

...When the short days of winter came (dusk) fell before we had well eaten our dinners. When we met in the street the houses had grown sombre. The space of sky above us was the colour of ever-changing violet and towards it the lamps of the street lifted their feeble lanterns.
5 The cold air stung us and we played till our bodies glowed. Our shouts echoed in the silent street. The career of our play brought us through the dark muddy lanes behind the houses where we ran the gauntlet of the rough tribes[1] from the cottages, to the back doors of the dark dripping gardens where odours arose from the ashpits, to the dark
10 odorous stables where a coachman smoothed and combed the horse or shook music from the buckled harness. When we returned to the street light from the kitchen windows had filled the areas. If my uncle was seen turning the corner we hid in the shadow until we had seen him safely housed. Or if Mangan's sister came out on the doorstep to
15 call her brother in to his tea we watched her from our shadow peer up and down the street. We waited to see whether she would remain or go in and, if she remained, we left our shadow and walked up to Mangan's steps resignedly. She was waiting for us, her figure defined by the light from the half-opened door. Her brother always teased her before he
20 obeyed and I stood by the railings looking at her. Her dress swung as she moved her body and the soft rope of her hair tossed from side to side.
Every morning I lay on the floor in the front parlour watching her door. The blind was pulled down to within an inch of the sash so that I could not be seen. When she came out on the doorstep my heart leaped. I
25 ran to the hall, seized my books and followed her. I kept her brown figure always in my eye and, when we came near the point at which our ways diverged, I quickened my pace and passed her. This happened morning after morning. I had never spoken to her, except for a few casual words, and yet her name was like a summons to all my foolish blood. ...
30 At last she spoke to me. When she addressed the first words to me I was so confused that I did not know what to answer. She asked me was I going to Araby. I forget whether I answered yes or no. It would be a splendid bazaar,[2] she said she would love to go.
'And why can't you?' I asked.

---

[1]tribes — gangs
[2]bazaar — fair

35   While she spoke she turned a silver bracelet round and round her wrist. She could not go, she said, because there would be a retreat[3] that week in her convent.[4] Her brother and two other boys were fighting for their caps and I was alone at the railings. She held one of the spikes, bowing her head towards me. The light from the lamp
40   opposite our door caught the white curve of her neck, lit up her hair that rested there and, falling, lit up the hand upon the railing. It fell over one side of her dress and caught the white border of a petticoat, just visible as she stood at ease.

'It's well for you,' she said.

45   'If I go,' I said, 'I will bring you something.'

What innumerable follies laid waste my waking and sleeping thoughts after that evening! I wished to annihilate the tedious intervening days. I chafed against the work of school. At night in my bedroom and by day in the classroom her image came between me and the page I
50   strove to read. The syllables of the word Araby were called to me through the silence in which my soul luxuriated and cast an Eastern enchantment over me. I asked for leave to go to the bazaar on Saturday night. My aunt was surprised and hoped it was not some Freemason[5] affair. I answered few questions in class. I watched my master's face pass
55   from amiability to sternness; he hoped I was not beginning to idle. I could not call my wandering thoughts together. I had hardly any patience with the serious work of life which, now that it stood between me and my desire, seemed to me child's play, ugly monotonous child's play.

60   On Saturday morning I reminded my uncle that I wished to go to the bazaar in the evening. He was fussing at the hallstand, looking for the hat-brush, and answered me curtly:

'Yes, boy, I know.' …

At nine o'clock I heard my uncle's latchkey in the halldoor. I heard
65   him talking to himself and heard the hallstand rocking when it had received the weight of his overcoat. I could interpret these signs. When he was midway through his dinner I asked him to give me the money to go to the bazaar. He had forgotten.

'The people are in bed and after their first sleep now,' he said.

70   I did not smile. My aunt said to him energetically: 'Can't you give him the money and let him go? You've kept him late enough as it is.' …

I held a florin[6] tightly in my hand as I strode down Buckingham Street towards the station. The sight of the streets thronged with buyers and glaring with gas recalled to me the purpose of my journey.
75   I took my seat in a third-class carriage of a deserted train. After an

---

[3]retreat — a time set aside for prayer and reflection
[4]convent — religious school
[5]Freemason — a fraternal organization
[6]florin — coin

intolerable delay the train moved out of the station slowly. It crept onward among ruinous houses and over the twinkling river. At Westland Row Station a crowd of people pressed to the carriage doors; but the porters moved them back, saying that it was a special train for the bazaar. I
80 remained alone in the bare carriage. In a few minutes the train drew up beside an improvised wooden platform. I passed out on to the road and saw by the lighted dial of a clock that it was ten minutes to ten. In front of me was a large building which displayed the magical name. ...

Remembering with difficulty why I had come I went over to one of
85 the stalls and examined porcelain vases and flowered tea-sets. At the door of the stall a young lady was talking and laughing with two young gentlemen. I remarked their English accents and listened vaguely to their conversation. ...

Observing me the young lady came over and asked me did I wish
90 to buy anything. The tone of her voice was not encouraging; she seemed to have spoken to me out of a sense of duty. I looked humbly at the great jars that stood like eastern guards at either side of the dark entrance to the stall and murmured:

'No, thank you.'
95 The young lady changed the position of one of the vases and went back to the two young men. They began to talk of the same subject. Once or twice the young lady glanced at me over her shoulder.

I lingered before her stall, though I knew my stay was useless, to make my interest in her wares seem the more real. Then I turned away
100 slowly and walked down the middle of the bazaar. I allowed the two pennies to fall against the sixpence in my pocket. I heard avoice call from one end of the gallery that the light was out. The upper part of the hall was now completely dark.

Gazing up into the darkness I saw myself as a creature driven and
105 derided by vanity; and my eyes burned with anguish and anger.

—James Joyce
excerpted from "Araby"
Dubliners, 1914
Grant Richards LTD.

1. The description of the neighborhood in lines 1 through 9 contributes to a mood of
(1) indifference   (2) gloom   (3) anxiety   (4) regret   1 ____

2. Which quotation from the text best illustrates the narrator's attitude toward Mangan's sister?
(1) "we watched her from our shadow" (line 15)
(2) "We waited to see whether she would remain or go in" (lines 16 and 17)
(3) "yet her name was like a summons" (line 29)
(4) "She asked me was I going to Araby" (lines 31 and 32)   2 ____

3. Lines 30 through 39 reveal Mangan's sister's
(1) disinterest   (2) silliness   (3) disappointment   (4) tension   3 ___

4. Lines 46 through 59 help to develop the idea that the narrator has
(1) recognized that his priorities have changed
(2) determined the academic focus of his studies
(3) eliminated distractions from his daily routine
(4) reassessed his relationship with his family   4 ___

5. The description of the narrator's train ride (lines 72 through 81) supports a theme of
(1) confusion   (2) isolation   (3) persecution   (4) deception   5 ___

6. The description in lines 89 through 99 suggests that the bazaar symbolizes
(1) excessive greed   (3) false promise
(2) future wealth   (4) lasting love   6 ___

7. It can be inferred from the text that the narrator's behavior is most guided by his
(1) school experience   (3) childhood memories
(2) family situation   (4) romantic feelings   7 ___

8. As used in line 105, the word "derided" most nearly means
(1) taunted   (2) restrained   (3) rewarded   (4) flattered   8 ___

9. Based on the text as a whole, the narrator's feelings of "anguish and anger" (line 105) are most likely a result of his having
(1) ignored his opportunities   (3) realized his limitations
(2) defended his family   (4) denied his responsibilities   9 ___

10. Which quotation best reflects a central theme of the text?
(1) "Her brother and two other boys were fighting for their caps" (lines 37 and 38)
(2) " 'Can't you give him the money and let him go?' "
(lines 70 and 71)
(3) "It crept onward among ruinous houses and over the twinkling river" (lines 76 and 77)
(4) "I lingered before her stall, though I knew my stay was useless" (line 98)   10 ___

Reading Comprehension Passage B
Assembly Line

In time's assembly line
Night presses against night.
We come off the factory night-shift
In line as we march towards home.
5   Over our heads in a row
The assembly line of stars
Stretches across the sky.
Beside us, little trees
Stand numb in assembly lines.

10   The stars must be exhausted
After thousands of years
Of journeys which never change.
The little trees are all sick,
Choked on smog and monotony,
15   Stripped of their color and shape.
It's not hard to feel for them;
We share the same tempo and rhythm.

Yes, I'm numb to my own existence
As if, like the trees and stars
20   —perhaps just out of habit
—perhaps just out of sorrow,
I'm unable to show concern
For my own manufactured fate.

—Shu Ting
from *A Splintered Mirror: Chinese Poetry from the Democracy Movement*, 1991
translated by Carolyn Kizer
North Point Press

11. In the first stanza, a main idea is strengthened through
the poet's use of
(1) repetition   (2) simile   (3) allusion   (4) understatement   11 ___

12. Line 17 contributes to a central idea by pointing out a parallel
between
(1) profit and industrialization   (3) recreation and production
(2) humans and nature   (4) sound and motion   12 ___

13. The structure and language of lines 20 and 21 suggests the narrator's
(1) bitterness   (2) determination   (3) selfishness   (4) uncertainty   13 ___

14. The phrase "manufactured fate" (line 23) emphasizes the narrator's
(1) resignation to life   (3) hope for change
(2) desire for control   (4) rejection of nature   14 ___

Reading Comprehension Passage C

...Memory teaches me what I know of these matters. The boy reminds the adult. I was a bilingual child, but of a certain kind: "socially disadvantaged," the son of working-class parents, both Mexican immigrants. ...

5   In public, my father and mother spoke a hesitant, accented, and not always grammatical English. And then they would have to strain, their bodies tense, to catch the sense of what was rapidly said by *los gringos*. At home, they returned to Spanish. The language of their Mexican past sounded in counterpoint to the English spoken in public. The words
10   would come quickly, with ease. Conveyed through those sounds was the pleasing, soothing, consoling reminder that one was at home.

     During those years when I was first learning to speak, my mother and father addressed me only in Spanish; in Spanish I learned to reply. By contrast, English (*inglés*) was the language I came to associate with
15   gringos, rarely heard in the house. I learned my first words of English overhearing my parents speaking to strangers. At six years of age, I knew just enough words for my mother to trust me on errands to stores one block away—but no more.

     I was then a listening child, careful to hear the very different sounds
20   of Spanish and English. Wide-eyed with hearing, I'd listen to sounds more than to words. First, there were English (gringo) sounds. So many words still were unknown to me that when the butcher or the lady at the drugstore said something, exotic polysyllabic sounds would bloom in the midst of their sentences. Often the speech of people in public
25   seemed to me very loud, booming with confidence. The man behind the counter would literally ask, "What can I do for you?" But by being so firm and clear, the sound of his voice said that he was a gringo; he belonged in public society. There were also the high, nasal notes of middle-class American speech—which I rarely am conscious of hearing
30   today because I hear them so often, but could not stop hearing when I was a boy. Crowds at Safeway or at bus stops were noisy with the birdlike sounds of *los gringos*. I'd move away from them all—all the chirping chatter above me.

     My own sounds I was unable to hear, but I knew that I spoke English
35   poorly. My words could not extend to form complete thoughts. And the words I did speak I didn't know well enough to make distinct sounds. (Listeners would usually lower their heads to hear better what I was trying to say). But it was one thing for *me* to speak English with difficulty; it was more troubling to hear my parents speaking in public: their
40   high-whining vowels and guttural[1] consonants; their sentences that got stuck with "eh" and "ah" sounds; the confused syntax; the hesitant rhythm of sounds so different from the way gringos spoke. I'd notice, moreover, that my parents' voices were softer than those of gringos we would meet.

---

[1]guttural — throaty

45   I am tempted to say now that none of this mattered. (In adulthood I am embarrassed by childhood fears.) And, in a way, it didn't matter very much that my parents could not speak English with ease. Their linguistic difficulties had no serious consequences. My mother and father made themselves understood at the county hospital clinic and at
50   government offices. And yet, in another way, it mattered very much. It was unsettling to hear my parents struggle with English. Hearing them, I'd grow nervous, and my clutching trust in their protection and power would be weakened. ...

But then there was Spanish: *español*, the language rarely heard away
55   from the house; *español*, the language which seemed to me therefore a private language, my family's language. To hear its sounds was to feel myself specially recognized as one of the family, apart from *los otros.*[2] A simple remark, an inconsequential comment could convey that assurance. My parents would say something to me and I would feel
60   embraced by the sounds of their words. Those sounds said: *I am speaking with ease in Spanish. I am addressing you in words I never use with los gringos. I recognize you as someone special, close, like no one outside. You belong with us. In the family. Ricardo.*

At the age of six, well past the time when most middle-class children
65   no longer notice the difference between sounds uttered at home and words spoken in public, I had a different experience. I lived in a world compounded of sounds. I was a child longer than most. I lived in a magical world, surrounded by sounds both pleasing and fearful. I shared with my family a language enchantingly private—different from that used
70   in the city around us. ...

If I rehearse here the changes in my private life after my Americanization, it is finally to emphasize a public gain. The loss implies the gain. The house I returned to each afternoon was quiet. Intimate sounds no longer greeted me at the door. Inside there were other
75   noises. The telephone rang. Neighborhood kids ran past the door of the bedroom where I was reading my schoolbooks—covered with brown shopping-bag paper. Once I learned the public language, it would never again be easy for me to hear intimate family voices. More and more of my day was spent hearing words, not sounds. But that may only
80   be a way of saying that on the day I raised my hand in class and spoke loudly to an entire roomful of faces, my childhood started to end. ...

—Richard Rodriguez
excerpted from "Aria: A Memoir of a Bilingual Childhood"
The American Scholar, Winter 1981
The Phi Beta Kappa Society

---

[2]los otros — the others

15. The phrase "the boy reminds the adult" in the first paragraph establishes the narrator's

(1) mood   (2) perspective   (3) creativity   (4) disposition   15 ____

16. The use of the word "counterpoint" in line 9 helps to develop a central idea by presenting

(1) differing memories   (3) contrasting cultures
(2) opposing principles   (4) conflicting philosophies   16 ____

17. The use of figurative language in line 20 demonstrates the narrator's

(1) eagerness to learn   (3) frustration with authority
(2) desire for recognition   (4) anxiety about adulthood   17 ____

18. The use of the word "public" in line 28 emphasizes the narrator's feeling of

(1) accomplishment   (3) satisfaction
(2) disillusionment   (4) separation   18 ____

19. The description of the narrator speaking English in lines 34 through 38 emphasizes his inability to

(1) communicate effectively   (3) distinguish between languages
(2) understand the culture   (4) express emotions   19 ____

20. In lines 47 through 53 the narrator's reaction to his parents' "linguistic difficulties" (line 48) reveals his

(1) low expectations   (3) educational concerns
(2) conflicting feelings   (4) hostile thoughts   20 ____

21. Lines 54 through 63 contribute to a central idea in the text by focusing on the

(1) narrator's sense of security   (3) family's traditional beliefs
(2) family's economic status   (4) narrator's feeling of confusion   21 ____

22. Which quotation best reflects the narrator's overall experience with language?

(1) "The words would come quickly, with ease" (lines 9 and 10)
(2) "I'd listen to sounds more than to words" (lines 20 and 21)
(3) "My own sounds I was unable to hear, but I knew that I spoke English poorly" (lines 34 and 35)
(4) "Hearing them, I'd grow nervous" (lines 51 and 52)   22 ____

23. The phrase "the loss implies the gain" (lines 72 and 73) contributes to a central idea in the text by indicating that when the narrator speaks English comfortably he is
(1) disconnected from his family
(2) distressed by hearing English sounds
(3) uninterested in his school work
(4) undeterred from making new friends   23 ___

24. The narrator's tone in lines 78 through 81 suggests
(1) distrust   (2) respect   (3) confidence   (4) intolerance   24 ___

Part 2
Argument
Directions: Closely read each of the *four* texts provided on the following pages and write a source-based argument on the topic below. You may use the margins to take notes as you read and scrap paper to plan your response. Write your argument on a separate sheet of paper provided by the teacher.

Topic: Should celebrities become the voice of humanitarian causes?

Your Task: Carefully read each of the *four* texts provided. Then, using evidence from at least *three* of the texts, write a well-developed argument regarding whether or not celebrities should become the voice of humanitarian causes. Clearly establish your claim, distinguish your claim from alternate or opposing claims, and use specific, relevant, and sufficient evidence from at least *three* of the texts to develop your argument. Do *not* simply summarize each text.

Guidelines:
   Be sure to:
   • Establish your claim regarding whether or not celebrities should become the voice of humanitarian causes
   • Distinguish your claim from alternate or opposing claims
   • Use specific, relevant, and sufficient evidence from at least *three* of the texts to develop your argument
   • Identify each source that you reference by text number and line number(s) or graphic (for example: Text 1, line 4 or Text 2, graphic)
   • Organize your ideas in a cohesive and coherent manner
   • Maintain a formal style of writing
   • Follow the conventions of standard written English

Texts:
   Text 1 – The Celebrity Solution
   Text 2 – Ethics of Celebrities and Their Increasing Influence
         in 21st Century Society
   Text 3 – Do Celebrity Humanitarians Matter?
   Text 4 – The Rise of the Celebrity Humanitarian Regents

Text 1
The Celebrity Solution

In 2004, Natalie Portman, then a 22-year-old fresh from college, went to Capitol Hill to talk to Congress on behalf of the Foundation for International Community Assistance, or Finca, a microfinance organization for which she served as "ambassador." She
5 found herself wondering what she was doing there, but her colleagues assured her: "We got the meetings because of you." For lawmakers, Natalie Portman was not simply a young woman — she was the beautiful Padmé from "Star Wars." "And I was like, 'That seems totally nuts to me,' " Portman told me recently. [*sic*] It's the way it works, I
10 guess. I'm not particularly proud that in our country I can get a meeting with a representative more easily than the head of a nonprofit can."

Well, who is? But it is the way it works. Stars — movie stars, rock stars, sports stars — exercise a ludicrous influence over the public
15 consciousness. Many are happy to exploit that power; others are wrecked by it. In recent years, stars have learned that their intense presentness in people's daily lives and their access to the uppermost realms of politics, business and the media offer them a peculiar kind of moral position, should they care to use it. And many of those with
20 the most leverage — Bono and Angelina Jolie and Brad Pitt and George Clooney and, yes, Natalie Portman — have increasingly chosen to mount that pedestal. Hollywood celebrities have become central players on deeply political issues like development aid, refugees and government-sponsored violence in Darfur.

25 Activists on these and other issues talk about the political power of stars with a mixture of bewilderment and delight. But a weapon that powerful is bound to do collateral damage. Some stars, like George Clooney, regard the authority thrust upon them with wariness; others, like Sean Penn or Mia Farrow, an activist on Darfur, seize the bully
30 pulpit with both hands. "There is a tendency," says Donald Steinberg, deputy president of the International Crisis Group, which seeks to prevent conflict around the world, "to treat these issues as if it's all good and evil." Sometimes you need the rallying cry, but sometimes you need to accept a complex truth. …

35 An entire industry has sprung up around the recruitment of celebrities to good works. Even an old-line philanthropy like the Red Cross employs a "director of celebrity outreach." Oxfam has a celebrity wrangler in Los Angeles, Lyndsay Cruz, on the lookout for stars who can raise the charity's profile with younger people. In addition to established figures
40 like Colin Firth and Helen Mirren, Oxfam is affiliated with Scarlett Johansson, who has visited South Asia (where the organization promotes girls' education) and is scheduled to go to Mali. Cruz notes

that while "trendy young people" are attracted to the star of "Match
Point" and "Lost in Translation," Johansson had "great credibility with
45 an older audience because she's such a great actress." ...

Microfinance is a one-star cause. Though for some reason the
subject appeals to female royalty, including Queen Rania of Jordan and
Princess Maxima of the Netherlands, Natalie Portman is the only
member of Hollywood royalty who has dedicated herself to it. Perhaps
50 this is because microfinance is a good deal more complicated than
supplying fresh water to parched villages, and a good deal less
glamorous than confronting the janjaweed[1] in Darfur. The premise of
microfinance is that very poor people should have access to credit, just
as the middle class and the rich do. They typically don't have such
55 access because banks that operate in the developing world view the
poor as too great a credit risk, and the processing cost of a $50 loan
is thought to wipe out much of the potential profit. But small nonprofit
organizations found that tiny loans could not only raise the incomes of
the rural and smalltown poor but also, unlike aid and other handouts,
60 could help make them self-sufficient. And they found as well that if
they harnessed the communities' own social bonds to create group
support, repayment rates among the very poor could be higher than
among the more well-off. (Indeed, commercial banks, apparently having
recognized their error, have now begun to extend loans to the poor.) The
65 idea of microfinance is thus to introduce the poor to capitalism. This is
not, it's true, star material. ...

There's no question that causes do a great deal for the brand identity
of the stars and the sponsors who embrace them. But what, exactly, do
stars do for causes? They raise money, of course. But that is often less
70 important than raising consciousness, as Natalie Portman has done.
John Prendergast, a longtime activist on African issues and the chairman
of Enough, an organization that brings attention to atrocities around the
world, says: "Celebrities are master recruiters. If you're trying to expand
beyond the already converted, there's no better way to do instant outreach
75 than to have a familiar face where people want to know more about
what they're doing in their personal lives." People come to see
Natalie Portman, and they go away learning about microfinance. ...

—James Traub
excerpted from "The Celebrity Solution"
www.nytimes.com, March 9, 2008

---

[1]janjaweed — militia

Text 2
Ethics of Celebrities and Their Increasing Influence
in 21st Century Society

The global influence of celebrities in the 21st century extends far beyond the entertainment sector. During the recent Palestinian presidential elections, the Hollywood actor Richard Gere broadcast a televised message to voters in the region and stated,

5   Hi, I'm Richard Gere, and I'm speaking for the entire world. (Richard Gere, actor)

Celebrities in the 21st century have expanded from simple product endorsements to sitting on United Nations committees, regional and global conflict commentators and international diplomacy. The Russian

10   parliament is debating whether to send a global celebrity to its International Space Station. The celebrities industry is undergoing, "mission creep", or the expansion of an enterprise beyond its original goals.

There has always been a connection between Hollywood and politics,

15   certainly in the USA. However, global celebrities in the 21st century are involved in proselytising[1] about particular religions, such as Scientology, negotiating with the Taliban in Afghanistan and participating in the Iraqi refugee crisis. The Hollywood actor, Jude Law's attempt to negotiate with the Taliban in Afghanistan was not

20   successful; but the mere fact that Jude Law tried, and that it was discussed widely over the global internet, shows the expansion of celebrities' domain in today's society. The global entertainment industry, especially based in Hollywood, has vastly exceeded their original mandate in society. ...

25   How is it that celebrities in the 21st century are formulating foreign aid policy, backing political bills or affecting public health debates? Traditionally, the economic value or market price of the entertainment industry and its various components was seen as intangible and difficult to measure. Movie stars and films, artists and the quality of art is often

30   seen as difficult to measure in terms of value and price without the role of expert opinions. But global internetdriven 21st century seems to be driven by a general growth of the idea that celebrity can be measured in a tangible way. ...

The 21st century's internet society seems to thrive on a harmonious

35   three-way relationship among celebrities, audiences and fame addiction. The global internet in turns [sic] moulds this three-way relationship and accelerates its dissemination[2] and communication. This in turn allows celebrities in the 21st century to "mission creep", or expand and accelerate their influence into various new areas of society. This interaction of

40   forces is shown in Figure 1. ...

---

[1]proselytising — trying to persuade or recruit others
[2]dissemination — wide distribution

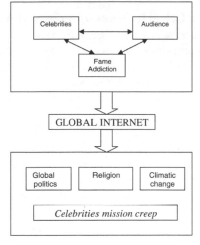

**Figure 1. Celebrities' mission creep
in the 21st century.**

In turn, the global popularity of internet-based social networking sites such as MySpace or individual blogspots all show the need to discuss events, but also things that are famous (Choi and Berger, 2009). Traditionally, celebrities were seen as people that needed to be seen
45 from afar and while keeping one's distance. In this sense, celebrities were similar to art pieces, better to be seen from a distance (Halpern, 2008; Hirsch, 1972; Maury and Kleiner, 2002). This traditional distance has been reduced due to global technologies in communications. Celebrities, and famous people in turn, help to bring people, including
50 adults, together in conversation and social interaction. The global role of the internet in the 21st century society will further accelerate such social and psychological trends throughout today's global knowledge-based society. Global internet communications have increased the availability of "fame" and access to the lives of celebrities, which in turn will
55 further accelerate the global influence of celebrities in the 21st century society. …

—Chong Ju Choi and Ron Berger
excerpted from "Ethics of Celebrities and
Their Increasing Influence in 21st Century Society"
Journal of Business Ethics, 2009
www.idc.ac.il

References

Choi, C.J. and R. Berger: 2009, 'Ethics of Internet, Global Community, Fame Addiction', *Journal of Business Ethics* (forthcoming).

Halpern, J.: 2008, *Fame Junkies* (Houghton Mifflin, New York).

Hirsch, P.: 1972, 'Processing Fads and Fashions: An Organisation Set Analysis of Cultural Industry Systems', *American Journal of Sociology* 77 (1), 45–70.

Maury, M. and D. Kleiner: 2002, 'E-Commerce, Ethical Commerce?', *Journal of Business Ethics* 36 (3), 21–32.

Text 3
Do Celebrity Humanitarians Matter?

...Recent years have seen a growth industry for celebrities engaged
in humanitarian activities. The website Look to the Stars has calculated
that over 2,000 charities have some form of celebrity support. UNICEF
has dozens of "Goodwill Ambassadors" and "Advocates" such as
5   Angelina Jolie and Mia Farrow. Celebrities have entered forums for
global governance to pressure political leaders: George Clooney has
spoken before the United Nations while Bob Geldof, Bono, and Sharon
Stone have attended summits like DAVOS[1] and the G8[2] to discuss third
world debt, poverty, and refugees. In the U.S. policy arena, [Ben]
10 Affleck joins Nicole Kidman, Angelina Jolie, and other celebrities who
have addressed the U.S. Congress on international issues.[3] The increase
in celebrity involvement has spurred debate in academic circles and
mainstream media. Celebrity humanitarianism is alternately lauded for
drawing media attention and fostering popular engagement and
15 criticized on a number of ethical grounds. According to Mother Jones,
Africa is experiencing a "recolonization" as celebrities from the U.S.
and UK lay claim to particular countries as recipients of their star
power: South Africa (Oprah), Sudan (Mia Farrow), and Botswana
(Russell Simmons). As the involvement of American celebrities in
20 humanitarian causes grows, let us consider the activities of Affleck and
his Eastern Congo Initiative [ECI].
Celebrity Humanitarians
      Affleck can be considered a "celebrity humanitarian," a celebrity figure
who has moved beyond his/her day job as an entertainer to delve into
25 the areas of foreign aid, charity, and development. These activities can
involve fundraising, hosting concerts and events, media appearances,
and engaging in advocacy. Celebrities are distinguished by their
unique ability to attract and engage diverse audiences ranging from their
fan base and the media to political elites and philanthropists. Celebrity
30 humanitarians often play an important bridging role, introducing
Northern publics to issues in the developing world. They also use their
star power to gain access to policy-making circles to effect social and
political change. Since 1980, the U.S. Congress has seen the frequency
of celebrity witnesses double to around 20 a year with most celebrity
35 appearances taking place before committees addressing domestic issues.
Interestingly, fewer than 5 percent of celebrity witnesses testify before
committees dealing with foreign relations, where celebrity humanitarians
push the United States to address global concerns.[4]

---

[1]DAVOS — an annual meeting of The World Economic Forum, hosted in Davos-Klosters,
Switzerland, on global partnership
[2]G8 — A group of 8 industrialized nations that hold a yearly meeting to discuss global issues
[3]ProQuest, "Quick Start: Congressional Hearing Digital Collections: Famous (Celebrity)
Witnesses," http://proquest.libguides.com/quick_start_hearings/famouscelebs
[4]See Demaine, L.J., n.d. Navigating Policy by the Stars: The Influence of Celebrity
Entertainers on Federal Lawmaking. Journal of Law & Politics, 25 (2), 83-143

The rise and influence of celebrity humanitarians activate debates
40 on the consequences of their involvement. For some academics and
practitioners, celebrities are welcome figures in humanitarianism:
educating the public on global issues, raising funds, and using their
populist appeal to draw attention to policy-making arenas. For others,
celebrity humanitarians are highly problematic figures who dilute
45 debates, offer misguided policy proposals, and lack credibility and
accountability. Celebrity humanitarianism privileges and invests the
celebrity figure with the responsibility of speaking on behalf of a "distant
other" who is unable to give input or consent for their representation.
Stakeholders in the developing world unwittingly rely on the celebrity
50 humanitarian as their communicator, advocate, and fundraiser. Finally,
celebrities are held to be self-serving, engaging in humanitarian causes to
burnish[5] their careers. ...

Celebrity humanitarians should do their homework to earn credibility
while also respecting their bounded roles as celebrity figures. As a
55 celebrity humanitarian, Affleck's proposals are based on serious
preparation: spending years to gain an in-depth understanding,
consulting with professionals, narrowing his advocacy efforts to a single
region, and enduring the scrutiny of the cameras and the blogosphere.
Besides this self-education, his credibility is based on ECI's dual mission
60 of re-granting and policymaking. Since ECI has operations and
partnerships in the DRC [Democratic Republic of the Congo], the
content of Affleck's writings and Congressional testimonies are grounded
in the realities of the DRC, peppered with first-hand accounts, and
supported by statistics and other research. However, there are limits to
65 his knowledge—Affleck is not a development expert or on-the-ground
professional;his day job and main career lie elsewhere. And while the
decision to found an organization suggests that Affleck's commitment
to the DRC will extend beyond his nascent[6] efforts, rumors that he
may seek political office distort this image.
70   Celebrity humanitarians must find a way to avoid diverting resources
and attention. Rather than bring his star power and ample financial support
to existing Congolese organizations, ECI furnished a platform for
Affleck's advocacy and leadership that amplifies his voice over those
of the Congolese. Nor was ECI crafted inside eastern Congo but in the
75 offices of a strategic advisory firm based in Seattle. ECI is privately
funded by a network of financial elites and does not rely on means-tested
grant cycles or public support. While Affleck has received multiple
awards in the short period he has been a celebrity humanitarian, his star
power also distracts us from the people who work in the field of
80 humanitarianism on a daily basis and rarely receive such recognition.[7]
And by concentrating attention and money for Affleck's issue of Eastern
Congo, other causes and countries may go unnoticed. ...

—Alexandra Cosima Budabin, excerpted and adapted from
"Do Celebrity Humanitarians Matter?" www.carnegiecouncil.org, December 11, 2014

---

[5]burnish — improve or enhance
[6]nascent — beginning
[7]Marina Hyde, "Angelina Jolie, Paris Hilton, Lassie and Tony Blair: here to save the world,"
The Guardian, 27 November 2014 http://www.theguardian.com/lifeandstyle/lostinshowbiz/2014/
nov/27/angelina-jolie-paris-hiltontony-

Text 4
The Rise of the Celebrity Humanitarian

...One of the most effective methods of attracting a wide, although perhaps not a deep, following is the use of a celebrity humanitarian: An A-Lister who has delved into areas of foreign aid, charity and international development. The United Nations is the leader in this

5 attention-getting ploy, with at least 175 celebrities on the books as goodwill ambassadors[1] for one cause or another. Some celebrities even leverage their star power to promote their very own foundations and philanthropic projects.

It's a mutually beneficial relationship, really. Hollywood's elite get to
10 wield their unique ability to engage diverse audiences, and the power of celebrity is put to good use effecting change—whether it's out of the good of their hearts, or because their publicists insist.

There is some downside that comes with publicly linking a campaign to a celebrity. For some, celebrity humanitarians are problematic figures[2]
15 who dilute debates, offer misguided policy proposals, and lack credibility and accountability. Take Scarlett Johansson, who became embroiled in a scandal after partnering with soft drink maker SodaStream, which operated a factory in occupied Palestinian territory. This alliance was in direct conflict with her sevenyear global ambassador position for
20 Oxfam, which opposes all trade with the occupied territories. In the end, she stepped down from her role with Oxfam, stating a fundamental difference of opinion.

Moreover, if the star's popularity takes a hit, it can affect the reception of the cause. For example, when Lance Armstrong's popularity
25 plummeted in the wake of doping allegations, it tarnished the brand of the Livestrong Foundation,[3] the nonprofit he founded to support people affected by cancer. Livestrong does, however, continue today, after cutting ties with Armstrong and undergoing a radical rebranding.

Even so, the following big names substantiate the idea that
30 celebrity involvement brings massive amounts of attention and money to humanitarian causes and that, usually, this [sic] is a good thing. ...

Bono participates in fundraising concerts like Live 8, and has co-founded several philanthropies, like the ONE Campaign and Product (RED). He also created EDUN, a fashion brand that strives to
35 stimulate trade in Africa by sourcing production there. He has received three nominations for the Nobel Peace Prize, was knighted by the United Kingdom in 2007, and was named Time's 2005 Person of the Year. ...

Popular singer Akon may not be as famous for his philanthropic work

---

[1]Bunting, Madeline. "The Issue of Celebrities and Aid Is Deceptively Complex"
http://www.theguardian.com, Dec. 17, 2010
[2]Budabin, Alexandra Cosima. "Do Celebrity Humanitarians Matter?"
http://www.carnegiecouncil.org, December 11, 2014
[3]Gardner, Eriq. "Livestrong Struggles After Lance Armstrong's Fall"
http://www.hollywoodreporter.com, 7/25/2013

as Angelina Jolie or Bono, but he is in a unique position to help, as he
40 has deep roots in the areas in which he works: He was raised in Senegal
in a community without electricity, which inspired his latest project,
Akon Lighting Africa. He also founded the Konfidence Foundation,
raising awareness of conditions in Africa and providing under privileged
African youth access to education and other resources. ...
45   In weighing the pros and cons of celebrity activism, perhaps [Ben]
Affleck himself summed it up best in an essay reflecting on the
constraints and possibilities of his own engagement:
"It makes sense to be skeptical about celebrity activism. There is
always suspicion that involvement with a cause may be doing more
50 good for the spokesman than he or she is doing for the cause...but
I hope you can separate whatever reservations you may have from
what is unimpeachably important."

—Jenica Funk
excerpted and adapted from "The Rise of the Celebrity Humanitarian"
www.globalenvision.org, January 29, 2015

Part 3
Text-Analysis Response

Your Task: Closely read the text provided on following pages and
write a well-developed, text-based response of two to three paragraphs. In
your response, identify a central idea in the text and analyze how the author's
use of *one* writing strategy (literary element or literary technique or
rhetorical device) develops this central idea. Use strong and thorough evidence
from the text to support your analysis. Do *not* simply summarize the text.
You may use the margins to take notes as you read and scrap paper to plan
your response. Write your response on a separate sheet of paper.

Guidelines:
Be sure to:
• Identify a central idea in the text
• Analyze how the author's use of *one* writing strategy (literary element
or literary technique or rhetorical device) develops this central idea.
Examples include: characterization, conflict, denotation/connotation,
metaphor, simile, irony, language use, point-of-view, setting, structure,
symbolism, theme, tone, etc.
• Use strong and thorough evidence from the text to support your analysis
• Organize your ideas in a cohesive and coherent manner
• Maintain a formal style of writing
• Follow the conventions of standard written English

Text

It was my father who called the city the Mansion on the River.

He was talking about Charleston, South Carolina, and he was a native son, peacock proud of a town so pretty it makes your eyes ache with pleasure just to walk down its spellbinding, narrow streets. Charleston was my
5 father's ministry, his hobbyhorse, his quiet obsession, and the great love of his life. His bloodstream lit up my own with a passion for the city that I've never lost nor ever will. I'm Charleston-born, and bred. The city's two rivers, the Ashley and the Cooper, have flooded and shaped all the days of my life on this storied[1] peninsula.

10   I carry the delicate porcelain beauty of Charleston like the hinged shell of some softtissued mollusk. My soul is peninsula-shaped and sun-hardened and river-swollen. The high tides of the city flood my consciousness each day, subject to the whims and harmonies of full moons rising out of the Atlantic. I grow calm when I see the ranks of
15 palmetto trees pulling guard duty on the banks of Colonial Lake or hear the bells of St. Michael's calling cadence[2] in the cicada-filled trees along Meeting Street. Deep in my bones, I knew early that I was one of those incorrigible[3] creatures known as Charlestonians. It comes to me as a surprising form of knowledge that my time in the city is
20 more vocation than gift; it is my destiny, not my choice. I consider it a high privilege to be a native of one of the loveliest American cities, not a high-kicking, glossy, or lipsticked city, not a city with bells on its fingers or brightly painted toenails, but a ruffled, low-slung city, understated and tolerant of nothing mismade or ostentatious.[4] Though Charleston
25 feels a seersuckered, tuxedoed view of itself, it approves of restraint far more than vainglory.[5]

    As a boy, in my own backyard I could catch a basket of blue crabs, a string of flounder, a dozen redfish, or a net full of white shrimp. All this I could do in a city enchanting enough to charm cobras out of baskets,
30 one so corniced and filigreed[6] and elaborate that it leaves strangers awed and natives self-satisfied. In its shadows you can find metalwork as delicate as lace and spiral staircases as elaborate as yachts. In the secrecy of its gardens you can discover jasmine and camellias and hundreds of other plants that look embroidered and stolen from the
35 Garden of Eden for the sheer love of richness and the joy of stealing from the gods. In its kitchens, the stoves are lit up in happiness as the lamb is marinating in red wine sauce, vinaigrette is prepared for the salad, crabmeat is anointed with sherry, custards are baked in the oven, and buttermilk biscuits cool on the counter.

40   Because of its devotional, graceful attraction to food and gardens and architecture, Charleston stands for all the principles that make living well both a civic virtue and a standard. It is a rapturous, defining place to grow up. Everything I reveal to you now will be Charleston-shaped and Charleston-governed, and sometimes even Charleston-ruined. But it

---

[1]storied — told of in history
[2]cadence — rhythmic recurrence of sound
[3]incorrigible — can not be reformed
[4]ostentatious — showy
[5]vainglory — excessive pride
[6]corniced and filigreed — architecturally decorated

45 is my fault and not the city's that it came close to destroying me. Not
everyone responds to beauty in the same way. Though Charleston can
do much, it can't always improve on the strangeness of human behavior.
But Charleston has a high tolerance for eccentricity and bemusement.[7]
There is a tastefulness in its gentility[8] that comes from the knowledge
50 that Charleston is a permanent dimple in the understated skyline, while
the rest of us are only visitors. ...

I turned out to be a late bloomer, which I long regretted. My parents
suffered needlessly because it took me so long to find my way to a place
at their table. But I sighted the early signs of my recovery long before
55 they did. My mother had given up on me at such an early age that
a comeback was something she no longer even prayed for in her wildest
dreams. Yet in my anonymous and underachieving high school career,
I laid the foundation for a strong finish without my mother noticing
that I was, at last, up to some good. I had built an impregnable castle
60 of solitude for myself and then set out to bring that castle down, no
matter how serious the collateral damage or who might get hurt.

I was eighteen years old and did not have a friend my own age. There
wasn't a boy in Charleston who would think about inviting me to a party
or to come out to spend the weekend at his family's beach house.
65 I planned for all that to change. I had decided to become the most
interesting boy to ever grow up in Charleston, and I revealed this secret
to my parents.

Outside my house in the languid[9] summer air of my eighteenth year,
I climbed the magnolia tree nearest to the Ashley River with the agility
70 that constant practice had granted me. From its highest branches, I
surveyed my city as it lay simmering in the hotblooded saps of June
while the sun began to set, reddening the vest of cirrus clouds that had
gathered along the western horizon. In the other direction, I saw the
city of rooftops and columns and gables that was my native land. What
75 I had just promised my parents, I wanted very much for them and
for myself. Yet I also wanted it for Charleston. I desired to turn myself
into a worthy townsman of such a many-storied city.

Charleston has its own heartbeat and fingerprint, its own mug shots
and photo ops and police lineups. It is a city of contrivance,[10] of
80 blueprints; devotion to pattern that is like a bent knee to the nature
of beauty itself. I could feel my destiny forming in the leaves high
above the city. Like Charleston, I had my alleyways that were dead
ends and led to nowhere, but mansions were forming like jewels in
my bloodstream. Looking down, I studied the layout of my city, the
85 one that had taught me all the lures of attractiveness, yet made me
suspicious of the showy or the makeshift. I turned to the stars and was
about to make a bad throw of the dice and try to predict the future, but
stopped myself in time.

A boy stopped in time, in a city of amber-colored life, that possessed
90 the glamour forbidden to a lesser angel. —Pat Conroy
excerpted from *South of Broad*, 2009, Nan A. Talese

---

[7]bemusement — bewilderment
[8]gentility — refinement
[9]languid — without energy
[10]contrivance — invention

ENGLISH Common Core Edition
August 2016
Part 1
Multiple-Choice Questions

Directions (1–24): Closely read each of the three passages below. After each passage, there are several multiple choice questions. Select the best suggested answer to each question and record your answer in the space provided. You may use the margins to take notes as you read.

Reading Comprehension Passage A

... Three years in London had not changed Richard, although it had changed the way he perceived the city. Richard had originally imagined London as a gray city, even a black city, from pictures he had seen, and he was surprised to find it filled with color. It was a city
5 of red brick and white stone, red buses and large black taxis, bright red mailboxes and green grassy parks and cemeteries ....

    Two thousand years before, London had been a little Celtic village on the north shore of the Thames, which the Romans had encountered, then settled in. London had grown, slowly, until, roughly a thousand years
10 later, it met the tiny Royal City of Westminster immediately to the west, and, once London Bridge had been built, London touched the town of Southwark directly across the river; and it continued to grow, fields and woods and marshland slowly vanishing beneath the flourishing town, and it continued to expand, encountering other little villages and hamlets
15 as it grew, like Whitechapel and Deptford to the east, Hammersmith and Shepherd's Bush to the west, Camden and Islington in the north, Battersea and Lambeth across the Thames to the south, absorbing all of them, just as a pool of mercury encounters and incorporates smaller beads of mercury, leaving only their names behind.
20   London grew into something huge and contradictory. It was a good place, and a fine city, but there is a price to be paid for all good places, and a price that all good places have to pay.

    After a while, Richard found himself taking London for granted; in time, he began to pride himself on having visited none of the sights of
25 London (except for the Tower of London, when his Aunt Maude came down to the city for a weekend, and Richard found himself her reluctant escort).

    But Jessica changed all that. Richard found himself, on otherwise sensible weekends, accompanying her to places like the National Gallery
30 and the Tate Gallery, where he learned that walking around museums too long hurts your feet, that the great art treasures of the world all blur into each other after a while, and that it is almost beyond the human capacity for belief to accept how much museum cafeterias will brazenly charge for a slice of cake and a cup of tea ....
35   Richard had been awed by Jessica, who was beautiful, and often quite funny, and was certainly going somewhere. And Jessica saw in Richard an enormous amount of potential, which, properly harnessed by the right woman, would have made him the perfect matrimonial accessory.

If only he were a little more focused, she would murmur to herself,
40 and so she gave him books with titles like *Dress for Success* and *A Hundred and Twenty-Five Habits of Successful Men*, and books on how to run a business like a military campaign, and Richard always said thank you, and always intended to read them. In Harvey Nichols's men's fashion department she would pick out for him the kinds of
45 clothes she thought that he should wear-and he wore them, during the week, anyway; and, a year to the day after their first encounter, she told him she thought it was time that they went shopping for an engagement ring.

"Why do you go out with her?" asked Gary, in Corporate Accounts,
50 eighteen months later. "She's terrifying."

Richard shook his head. "She's really sweet, once you get to know her."

Gary put down the plastic troll doll he had picked up from Richard's desk. I'm surprised she still lets you play with these." ...
55   It was a Friday afternoon. Richard had noticed that events were cowards: they didn't occur singly, but instead they would run in packs and leap out at him all at once. Take this particular Friday, for example. It was, as Jessica had pointed out to him at least a dozen times in the last month, the most important day of his life. So it was unfortunate
60 that, despite the Post-it note Richard had left on his fridge door at home, and the other Post-it note he had placed on the photograph of Jessica on his desk, he had forgotten about it completely and utterly.

Also, there was the Wandsworth report, which was overdue and taking up most of his head. Richard checked another row of figures;
65 then he noticed that page 17 had vanished, and he set it up to print out again; and another page down, and he knew that if he were only left alone to finish it .. .if, miracle of miracles, the phone did not ring .... It rang. He thumbed the speakerphone.

"Hello? Richard? The managing director needs to know when he'll
70 have the report."

Richard looked at his watch. "Five minutes, Sylvia. It's almost wrapped up. I just have to attach the P & L projection."

"Thanks, Dick. I'll come down for it." Sylvia was, as she liked to explain, "the MD's PA," [Managing Director's Personal Assistant] and
75 she moved in an atmosphere of crisp efficiency. He thumbed the speakerphone off; it rang again, immediately. "Richard," said the speaker, with Jessica's voice, "it's Jessica. You haven't forgotten, have you?"

"Forgotten?" He tried to remember what he could have forgotten. He looked at Jessica's photograph for inspiration and found all the
80 inspiration he could have needed in the shape of a yellow Post-it note stuck to her forehead.

"Richard? Pick up the telephone."

He picked up the phone, reading the Post-it note as he did so. "Sorry, Jess. No, I hadn't forgotten. Seven P.M., at Ma Maison Italiano. Should
85 I meet you there?"

"Jessica, Richard. Not Jess." She paused for a moment. "Ater what happened last time? I don't think so. You really could get lost in your own backyard, Richard." ...

"I'll meet you at your place," said Jessica. 'We can walk down together."

90   "Right, Jess. Jessica-sorry."

"You *have* confirmed our reservation, haven't you, Richard."

"Yes," lied Richard earnestly. The other line on his phone had begun to ring. "Jessica, look, I..."

"Good," said Jessica, and she broke the connection. He picked up
95 the other line.

"Hi Dick. It's me, Gary." Gary sat a few desks down from Richard. He waved. "Are we still on for drinks? You said we could go over the Merstham account."

"Get off the bloody phone, Gary. Of course we are." Richard put
100 down the phone. There was a telephone number at the bottom of the Post-it note; Richard had written the Post-it note to himself, several weeks earlier. And he *had* made the reservation: he was almost certain of that. But he had not confirmed it. He had kept meaning to, but there had been so much to do and Richard had known that there was plenty
105 of time. But events run in packs ...

Sylvia was now standing next to him. "Dick? The Wandsworth report?"

"Almost ready, Sylvia. Look, just hold on a sec, can you?"

He finished punching in the number, breathed a sigh of relief when
110 somebody answered. "Ma Maison. Can I help you?"

"Yes," said Richard. "A table for three, for tonight. I think I booked it. And if I did I'm confirming the reservation. And if I didn't, I wondered if I could book it. Please." No, they had no record of a table for tonight in the name of Mayhew. Or Stockton. Or Bartram—Jessica's
115 surname. And as for booking a table ...

They had put down the phone.

"Richard?" said Sylvia. "The MD's waiting."

"Do you think," asked Richard, "they'd give me a table if I phoned back and offered them extra money?" ...

-Neil Gaiman
excerpted and adapted from *Neverwhere,* 1997
Avon Books

1. The author most likely includes the description of London in lines 1 through 22 to
(1) provide reasons for Richard's dislike of the city
(2) highlight opportunities for Richard's career in the city
(3) convey a sense of Richard's frustration with the city
(4) illustrate the nature of Richard's life in the city   1 _____

2. The figurative language used in line 18 reinforces the
(1) growth of the city   (3) increase in isolation
(2) problems with development   (4) history of the towns   2 _____

3. The narrator uses lines 28 through 34 to help the reader understand Richard's
(1) continuous efforts to save money while on dates
(2) willingness to tolerate undesirable situations to please others
(3) overall acceptance of cultural experiences in the city
(4) affection for newfound experiences when shared with others   3 ____

4. In the context of the text as a whole, which statement regarding lines 49 through 52 is true?
(1) Gary is jealous of Richard because he has a girlfriend.
(2) Gary has a moody temperament and hides his feelings.
(3) Richard has a plan and wishes to keep it a secret.
(4) Richard is in a state of denial regarding his relationship.   4 ____

5. How do lines 55 to 57 contribute to the characterization of Richard?
(1) by portraying him as inefficient at organizing his time
(2) by indicating that he works well under pressure
(3) by describing him as likely to succeed
(4) by suggesting that he is unmotivated in his job   5 ____

6. The narrator's description of Sylvia as moving "in an atmosphere of crisp efficiency" (line 75) presents a
(1) shift   (2) possibility   (3) contrast   (4) solution   6 ____

7. Lines 82 through 87 contribute to a central idea by highlighting Jessica's
(1) domineering nature   (3) lack of responsibility
(2) compassionate side   (4) sense of humor   7 ____

8. The narrator's use of dialogue in lines 82 through 100 enhances a mood of
(1) satisfaction   (2) stress   (3) confidence   (4) remorse   8 ____

9. Richard's question in lines 118 and 119 reveals his
(1) subtle refinement   (3) honest gratitude
(2) suppressed hostility   (4) quiet desperation   9 ____

10. Which quote best reflects a central theme in the text?
(1) "London grew into something huge and contradictory ... and a price that all good places have to pay." (lines 20 through 22)
(2) "Richard checked another row of figures ... and he set it up to print out again;" (lines 64 through 66)
(3) "Richard looked at his watch. 'Five minutes, Sylvia. It's almost wrapped up. I just have to attach the P & L projection.' " (lines 71 and 72)
(4) "He finished punching in the number, breathed a sigh of relief when somebody answered. 'Ma Maison. Can I help you?' " (lines 109 and 110)
10 ____

Reading Comprehension Passage B
We Are Many

Of the many men whom I am, whom we are,
I cannot settle on a single one.
They are lost to me under the cover of clothing.
They have departed for another city.

5   When everything seems to be set
to show me off as a man of intelligence,
the fool I keep concealed on my person
takes over my talk and occupies my mouth.

On other occasions, I am dozing in the midst
10   of people of some distinction,
and when I summon my courageous self,
a coward completely unknown to me
swaddles[1] my poor skeleton
in a thousand tiny reservations.

15   When a stately home bursts into flames,
instead of the fireman I summon,
an arsonist bursts on the scene,
and he is I. There is nothing I can do.
What must I do to distinguish myself?
20   How can I put myself together?

All the books I read
lionize[2] dazzling hero figures,
always brimming with self-assurance.
I die with envy of them;
25   and, in films where bullets fly on the wind,
I am left in envy of the cowboys,
left admiring even the horses.

But when I call upon my dashing being,
out comes the same old lazy self,
30   and so I never know just who I am,
nor how many I am, nor who we will be being.
I would like to be able to touch a bell
and call up my real self, the truly me,
because if I really need my proper self,
35   I must not allow myself to disappear.

---

[1]swaddles — wraps
[2]lionize -- glorify

While I am writing, I am far away;
and when I come back, I have already left.
I should like to see if the same thing happens
to other people as it does to me,
40 to see if as many people are as I am,
and if they seem the same way to themselves.
When this problem has been thoroughly explored,
I am going to school myself so well in things
that, when I try to explain my problems,
45 I shall speak, not of self, but of geography.

-Pablo Neruda
from *We Are Many*, 1970
translated by Alastair Reid
Grossman Publishers

11. The overall purpose of the figurative language in lines 12 through 14 is
to show the narrator's
(1) contempt for self-reliance   (3) lack of self-confidence
(2) desire for adventure   (4) jealousy of writers   11 ___

12. A primary function of the questions in lines 19 and 20 is to
(1) introduce the narrator's biases
(2) challenge the narrator's beliefs
(3) clarify the narrator's dilemma
(4) explain the narrator's decision   12 ___

13. The contradictions presented throughout the poem serve to
illustrate the relationship between
(1) society's conflicts and the narrator's reaction
(2) the narrator's sensibilities and his determination
(3) society's expectations and the narrator's possibilities
(4) the narrator's idealism and his reality   13 ___

14. The solution proposed in lines 42 through 45 can best be
described as
(1) balanced   (2) universal   (3) inappropriate   (4) unrealistic   14 ___

... By natural design, dogs' ears have evolved to hear certain kinds of
sounds. Happily, that set of sounds overlaps with those we can hear
and produce: if we utter it, it will at least hit the eardrum of a nearby
dog. Our auditory range is from 20 hertz to 20 kilohertz: from the lowest
5   pitch on the longest organ pipe to an impossibly squeaky squeak. We
spend most of our time straining to understand sounds between
100 hertz and 1 kilohertz, the range of any interesting speech going on
in the vicinity. Dogs hear most of what we hear and then some. They
can detect sounds up to 45 kilohertz, much higher than the hair cells of
10   our ears bother to bend to. Hence the power of the dog whistle, a
seemingly magical device that makes no apparent sound and yet perks
the ears of dogs for blocks around. We call this sound "ultrasonic,"
since it's beyond our ken,[1] but it is within the sonic range for many
animals in our local environment. Don't think for a moment that
15   apart from the occasional dog whistle, the world is quiet for dogs
up at those high registers. Even a typical room is pulsing with high
frequencies, detectable by dogs constantly. Think your bedroom is quiet
when you rise in the morning? The crystal resonator used in digital
alarm clocks emits a never-ending alarm of high-frequency pulses
20   audible to canine ears. Dogs can hear the navigational chirping of
rats behind your walls and the bodily vibrations of termites within your
walls. That compact fluorescent light you installed to save energy? You
may not hear the hum, but your dog probably can.

    The range of pitches we are most intent on are those used in speech.
25   Dogs hear all sounds of speech, and are nearly as good as we are at
detecting a change of pitch-relevant, say, for understanding statements,
which end in a low pitch, versus questions, which in English end in
a raised pitch: "Do you want to go for a walk(?)" With the question
mark, this sentence is exciting to a dog with experience going on walks
30   with humans. Without it, it is simply noise. Imagine the confusion
generated by the recent growth of "up-talking," speech that ends every
sentence with the sound of a question?

    If dogs understand the stress and tones-the *prosody*-of speech, does
this hint that they understand language? This is a natural but vexed[2]
35   question. Since language use is one of the most glaring differences
between the human animal and all other animals, it has been
proposed as the ultimate, incomparable criterion for intelligence. This
raises serious hackles[3] in some animal researchers (not thought of as
a hackled species, ironically), who have set about trying to demonstrate

---

[1]ken — recognition
[2]vexed — problematic
[3]raises serious hackles — arouses anger

40 what linguistic ability animals have. Even those researchers who may agree that language is necessary for intelligence have nonetheless added reams of results to the growing pile of evidence of linguistic ability in non-human animals. All parties agree, though, that there has been no discovery of a humanlike language-a corpus[4] of infinitely combinable
45 words that often carry many definitions, with rules for combining words into meaningful sentences-in animals.

This is not to say that animals might not understand some of our language use, even if they don't produce it themselves. There are, for instance, many examples of animals taking advantage of the
50 communicative system of nearby unrelated animal species. Monkeys can make use of nearby birds' warning calls of a nearby predator to themselves take protective action. Even an animal who deceives another animal by mimicry-which some snakes, moths, and even flies can do-is in some way using another species's [*sic*] language.

55 The research with dogs suggests that they do understand language-to a limited degree. On the one hand, to say that dogs understand *words* is a misnomer. Words exist in a language, which itself is product of a culture; dogs are participants in that culture on a very different level. Their framework for understanding the application of the word is entirely
60 different. There is, no doubt, more to the words of their world than Gary Larson's *Far Side* comics suggest: eat, walk, and fetch. But he is on to something, insofar as these are organizing elements of their interaction with us: we circumscribe the dog's world to a small set of activities. Working dogs seem miraculously responsive and focused compared to
65 city pets. It is not that they are innately more responsive or focused, but that their owners have added to their vocabularies types of things to do.

One component in understanding a word is the ability to discriminate it from other words. Given their sensitivity to the prosody of speech, dogs do not always excel at this. Try asking your dog on one morning to *go for*
70 *a walk*; on the next, ask if your dog wants to *snow forty locks* in the same voice. If everything else remains the same, you'll probably get the same, affirmative reaction. The very first sounds of an utterance seem to be important to dog perception, though, so changing the swallowed consonants for articulated ones and the long vowels for short ones-*ma*
75 *for a polk?*-might prompt the confusion merited by this gibberish. Of course humans read meaning into prosody, too. English does not give the prosody of speech syntactical leverage but it is still part of how we interpret "what has just been said."

If we were more sensitive to the *sound* of what we say to dogs, we
80 might get better responses from them. High-pitched sounds mean something different than low sounds; rising sounds contrast with falling sounds. It is not accidental that we find ourselves cooing to an infant

---

[4]corpus — collection

in silly, giddy tones (called *motherese*)-and might greet a wagging dog
with similar baby talk. Infants can hear other speech sounds, but they
85   are more interested in motherese. Dogs, too, respond with alacrity[5] to
baby talk-partially because it distinguishes speech that is directed *at*
them from the rest of the continuous yammering above their heads.
Moreover, they will come more easily to high-pitched and repeated
call requests than to those at a lower pitch. What is the ecology behind
90   this? High-pitched sounds are naturally interesting to dogs: they might
indicate the excitement of a tussle or the shrieking of nearby injured
prey. If a dog fails to respond to your reasonable suggestion that he
come *right now*, resist the urge to lower and sharpen your tone. It
indicates your frame of mind- and the punishment that might ensue for
95   his prior uncooperativeness. Correspondingly, it is easier to get a dog to
sit on command to a longer, descending tone rather than repeated, rising
notes. Such a tone might be more likely to induce relaxation, or
preparation for the next command from their talky human ....

–Alexandra Horowitz
excerpted from *Inside of a Dog*, 2010
Scribner

---

[5]alacrity — eagerness

15. Lines 1 through 14 introduce the central idea of the passage by
(1) explaining how ear structure affects sound
(2) describing various frequencies dogs hear
(3) explaining various ways humans hear
(4) describing how dog whistle tones differ   15 ___

16. Lines 24 through 28 best support the idea that
(1) dogs cannot learn to obey human signals
(2) human actions are difficult for dogs to interpret
(3) humans can verbally communicate with dogs
(4) dogs can learn complex human language   16 ___

17. Based on lines 24 through 32, humans can possibly confuse dogs by
(1) speaking to dogs in a nonsense language
(2) giving dogs only direct commands
(3) making gestures when speaking to dogs
(4) altering the intonation of familiar words   17 ___

18. Lines 33 through 38 illustrate that language use is an indicator of
(1) higher-level thinking   (3) increased emotional response
(2) basic survival instinct   (4) problem-solving skills   18 ___

19. In lines 43 through 46, the author states there is agreement
that non-human animals cannot
(1) master complicated directions
(2) duplicate human sound pitches
(3) create human sentence structures
(4) interpret foreign languages   19 ___

20. The primary function of the examples in lines 48 through 54
is to show how some animals can
(1) imitate behavior and sound
(2) foster community and diversity
(3) transform from prey to predator
(4) compromise freedom for safety   20 ___

21. The author uses the term "gibberish" in line 75 to emphasize the
(1) importance of word order
(2) complexity of spoken sounds
(3) relevance of hidden gestures
(4) necessity of voice and movement   21 ___

22. Which sentence best restates a central idea in lines 72 through 82?
(1) High-pitched sounds often cause dogs to become agitated.
(2) How we speak to dogs is more important than what we say.
(3) Dogs must learn to interpret human speech early in life.
(4) Dogs become distressed when they hear baby talk.   22 ___

23. The author's reference to "motherese" (line 83) helps to illustrate
a connection between the
(1) combinations of languages and the effects on listeners
(2) volume of speech and possible misperception
(3) importance of word choice and its impact on understanding
(4) styles of spoken communication and likely responses   23 ___

24. The primary purpose of the text is to
(1) explain a popular myth regarding dogs' behavior
(2) promote a new method for working with dogs
(3) educate people about dogs' experience with sound
(4) present an alternative to traditional dog training   24 ___

Part 2
Argument
Directions: Closely read each of the *four* texts provided on the following pages and write a source-based argument on the topic below. You may use the margins to take notes as you read and scrap paper to plan your response. Write your argument on a separate sheet of paper provided by the teacher.

Topic: Should the United States government create strict sugar regulations?

Your Task: Carefully read each of the *four* texts provided. Then, using evidence from at least *three* of the texts, write a well-developed argument regarding whether or not the United States government should create strict sugar regulations. Clearly establish your claim, distinguish your claim from alternate or opposing claims, and use specific, relevant, and sufficient evidence from at least *three* of the texts to develop your argument. Do *not* simply summarize each text.

Guidelines:
Be sure to:
• Establish your claim regarding whether or not the United States government should create strict sugar regulations

• Distinguish your claim from alternate or opposing claims

• Use specific, relevant, and sufficient evidence from at least *three* of the texts to develop your argument

• Identify each source that you reference by text number and line number(s) or graphic (for example: Text 1, line 4 or Text 2, graphic)

• Organize your ideas in a cohesive and coherent manner

• Maintain a formal style of writing

• Follow the conventions of standard written English

Texts:
Text 1 – FDA Urged to Regulate Sugar in Drinks
Text 2 – Sugar Should Be Regulated As Toxin, Researchers Say
Text 3 – The Toxic Truth About Sugar
Text 4 – Sugar Taxes Are Unfair and Unhealthy

Text 1
FDA Urged to Regulate Sugar in Drinks

WASHINGTON — The US Food and Drug Administration [FDA] should regulate the amount of added sugars in soda and other sweetened beverages to reverse the obesity epidemic, a Washington-based nutrition activist group urged in a petition signed by Harvard School of Public
5   Health researchers, the Boston Public Health Commission, and others.
    "The FDA considers sugar to be a safe food at the recommended level of consumption, but Americans are consuming two to three times that much," Michael Jacobson, executive director of the Center for Science in the Public Interest, which filed the petition, said at a press briefing on
10   Wednesday. He added that the average American consumes 78 pounds of added sugars each year, mostly from high fructose corn syrup prevalent in sugary sodas, sports drinks, and fruit punch. ...
    Over the past half-century, Americans have dramatically increased their intake of sugary drinks, and research suggests this has contributed
15   to the obesity epidemic and a rise in related diseases such as type 2 diabetes, heart disease, and a variety of cancers.
    "The evidence is very robust that when we eat more sugar we gain weight and when we eat less, we lose weight," said Dr. Walter Willett, chairman of nutrition at the Harvard School of Public Health, who also
20   spoke at the briefing. "Each 12-ounce serving of soda a person consumes each day raises type 2 diabetes risk by 10 to 15 percent, and many Americans are consuming five or six servings."
    While the FDA has the authority to set limits on ingredients on its "generally recognized as safe" list, it has not done so for many of them,
25   including table sugar and high fructose corn syrup.
    Jeffrey Senger, former acting chief counsel of the FDA who is now a partner at the law firm Sidley Austin, said it is unlikely the agency would act to restrict sugar. "Any food, if it's abused, can be unhealthy," he said. "Sugar isn't the same thing as arsenic. It's not a food that's inherently
30   unsafe." ...
    She [FDA spokeswoman, Shelly Burgess] confirmed that the latest petition was received and would be reviewed by FDA officials, but added that the FDA was not aware of any evidence highlighting added safety risks from high fructose corn syrup compared with other sugars such
35   as honey, table sugar, or molasses.
    That suggests that the agency might have a hard time requiring Coke or Pepsi to limit their products to 10 grams of added sugar per serving — what many public health specialists recommend — without also requiring the same limits on cereal, baked goods, and other processed foods.
40   "To limit the amount of added sugars in beverages, the FDA would need to establish that there is enough scientific evidence to justify limiting these ingredients and to go through a rulemaking process that allows for public comment," said Miriam Guggenheim, a partner in the food and beverage practice at Covington & Burling LLP in

45   Washington, D.C.
         Taking a firm position against government regulations to limit added
     sugars, the American Beverage Association, which represents soft drink
     manufacturers, pointed out in a statement on its website that companies
     have already made efforts to reduce sugar in sweetened beverages.
50   "Today about 45 percent of all non-alcoholic beverages purchased
     have zero calories," the group said, "and the overall average number of
     calories per beverage serving is down 23 percent since 1998." ...
         About half of Americans consume sugary beverages on any given
     day, according to the latest data from the federal Centers for Disease
55   Control and Prevention, and consumption of sugary beverages has
     increased among children and adults over the past 30 years.

—Deborah Kotz
excerpted and adapted from "FDA Urged to Regulate Sugar in Drinks"
http://www.bostonglobe.com, February 14, 2013

Text 2
Sugar Should Be Regulated As Toxin, Researchers Say
         A spoonful of sugar might make the medicine go down. But it also
     makes blood pressure and cholesterol go up, along with your risk for
     liver failure, obesity, heart disease and diabetes.
         Sugar and other sweeteners are, in fact, so toxic to the human body
5   that they should be regulated as strictly as alcohol by governments
     worldwide, according to a commentary in the current issue of the
     journal Nature by researchers at the University of California, San
     Francisco (UCSF).
         The researchers propose regulations such as taxing all foods and
10   drinks that include added sugar, banning sales in or near schools and
     placing age limits on purchases.
         Although the commentary might seem straight out of the Journal of
     Ideas That Will Never Fly, the researchers cite numerous studies and
     statistics to make their case that added sugar — or, more specifically,
15   sucrose, an even mix of glucose and fructose found in highfructose
     corn syrup and in table sugar made from sugar cane and sugar beets —
     has been as detrimental to society as alcohol and tobacco.

Sour words about sugar

         ...Many researchers are seeing sugar as not just "empty calories," but
     rather a chemical that becomes toxic in excess. At issue is the fact
20   that glucose from complex carbohydrates, such as whole grains, is
     safely metabolized by cells throughout the body, but the fructose
     element of sugar is metabolized primarily by the liver. This is where
     the trouble can begin — taxing the liver, causing fatty liver disease,
     and ultimately leading to insulin resistance, the underlying causes of

25   obesity and diabetes.

Added sugar, more so than the fructose in fiber-rich fruit, hits the liver more directly and can cause more damage — in laboratory rodents, anyway. Some researchers, however, remained unconvinced of the evidence of sugar's toxic effect on the human body at current
30   consumption levels, as high as they are.

Economists to the rescue

[Robert] Lustig, a medical doctor in UCSF's Department of Pediatrics, compares added sugar to tobacco and alcohol (coincidentally made from sugar) in that it is addictive, toxic and has a negative impact on society, thus meeting established public health criteria for regulation.
35   Lustig advocates a consumer tax on any product with added sugar.

Among Lustig's more radical proposals are to ban the sale of sugary drinks to children under age 17 and to tighten zoning laws for the sale of sugary beverages and snacks around schools and in low-income areas plagued by obesity, analogous to alcoholism and alcohol regulation.
40   Economists, however, debate as to whether a consumer tax — such as a soda tax proposed in many U.S. states — is the most effective means of curbing sugar consumption. Economists at Iowa State University led by John Beghin suggest taxing the sweetener itself at the manufacturer level, not the end product containing sugar.
45   This concept, published last year in the journal Contemporary Economic Policy, would give companies an incentive to add less sweetener to their products. After all, high-fructose corn syrup is ubiquitous[1] in food in part because it is so cheap and serves as a convenient substitute for more high-quality ingredients, such as fresher
50   vegetables in processed foods.

Some researchers argue that saturated fat, not sugar, is the root cause of obesity and chronic disease. Others argue that it is highly processed foods with simple carbohydrates. Still others argue that it is a lack of physical exercise. It could, of course, be a matter of all these issues.

—Christopher Wanjek
excerpted and adapted from "Sugar Should Be Regulated As Toxin,
Researchers Say"
http://www.livescience.com, February 1, 2012

---

[1]ubiquitous — present everywhere

Text 3
The Toxic Truth About Sugar
...No Ordinary Commodity

In 2003, social psychologist Thomas Babor and his colleagues published a landmark book called *Alcohol: No Ordinary Commodity*, in which they established four criteria, now largely accepted by the public-health community, that justify the regulation of alcohol —

5   unavoidability (or pervasiveness throughout society), toxicity, potential for abuse and negative impact on society. Sugar meets the same criteria, and we believe that it similarly warrants some form of societal intervention.

First, consider unavoidability. Evolutionarily, sugar as fruit was
10 available to our ancestors for only a few months a year (at harvest time), or as honey, which was guarded by bees. But in recent years, sugar has been added to virtually every processed food, limiting consumer choice. Nature made sugar hard to get; man made it easy. In many parts of the world, people are consuming an average of more than 500 calories
15 per day from added sugar alone.

Now, let's consider toxicity. A growing body of epidemiological and mechanistic[1] evidence argues that excessive sugar consumption affects human health beyond simply adding calories. Importantly, sugar induces all of the diseases associated with metabolic syndrome. This includes:
20 hypertension (fructose increases uric acid, which raises blood pressure); high triglycerides and insulin resistance through synthesis of fat in the liver; diabetes from increased liver glucose production combined with insulin resistance; and the ageing process, caused by damage to lipids, proteins and DNA [deoxyribonucleic acid] through non-
25 enzymatic binding of fructose to these molecules. It can also be argued that fructose exerts toxic effects on the liver similar to those of alcohol. This is no surprise, because alcohol is derived from the fermentation of sugar. Some early studies have also linked sugar consumption to human cancer and cognitive decline.

30 Sugar also has a clear potential for abuse. Like tobacco and alcohol, it acts on the brain to encourage subsequent intake. There are now numerous studies examining the dependence-producing properties of sugar in humans. Specifically, sugar dampens the suppression of the hormone ghrelin, which signals hunger to the brain. It also interferes
35 with the normal transport and signalling of the hormone leptin, which helps to produce the feeling of satiety.[2] And it reduces dopamine signalling in the brain's reward centre, thereby decreasing the pleasure derived from food and compelling the individual to consume more.

[1]epidemiological and mechanistic — evidence based on the study of the causes, incidence, and treatment of diseases
[2]satiety — fullness

Finally, consider the negative effects of sugar on society. Passive
40 smoking and drink-driving fatalities provided strong arguments for
tobacco and alcohol control, respectively. The long-term economic,
health-care and human costs of metabolic syndrome place sugar
overconsumption in the same category. The United States spends
$65 billion in lost productivity and $150 billion on health-care
45 resources annually for co-morbidities[3] associated with metabolic
syndrome. Seventy-five per cent of all US health-care dollars are now
spent on treating these diseases and resultant disabilities. Because
75% of military applicants are now rejected for obesity-related reasons,
the past three US surgeons general and the chairman of the US Joint
50 Chiefs of Staff have declared obesity a "threat to national security".

How to Intervene

How can we reduce sugar consumption? After all, sugar is natural.
Sugar is a nutrient. Sugar is pleasure. So is alcohol, but in both cases,
too much of a good thing is toxic. It may be helpful to look to the
many generations of international experience with alcohol and tobacco
55 to find models that work. So far, evidence shows that individually focused
approaches, such as school-based interventions that teach children about
diet and exercise, demonstrate little efficacy.[4] Conversely, for both
alcohol and tobacco, there is robust evidence that gentle 'supply
side' control strategies which stop far short of all-out prohibition —
60 taxation, distribution controls, age limits — lower both consumption
of the product and accompanying health harms. Successful interventions
all share a common end-point: curbing availability. ...

DEADLY EFFECT Excessive consumption of fructose can cause many of the same health problems as alcohol.	
Chronic ethanol exposure	**Chronic fructose exposure**
Hematologic disorders	
Electrolyte abnormalities	
Hypertension	Hypertension (uric acid)
Cardiac dilatation	
Cardiomyopathy	Myocardial infarction (dyslipidemia, insulin resistance)
Dyslipidemia	Dyslipidemia (de novo lipogenesis)
Pancreatitis	Pancreatitis (hypertriglyceridemia)
Obesity (insulin resistance)	Obesity (insulin resistance)
Malnutrition	Malnutrition (obesity)
Hepatic dysfunction (alcoholic steatohepatitis)	Hepatic dysfunction (non-alcoholic steatohepatitis)
Fetal alcohol syndrome	
Addiction	Habituation, if not addiction

[3]co-morbidities — diseases that occur simultaneously
[4]efficacy — power to produce an effect

The Possible Dream

Government-imposed regulations on the marketing of alcohol to young people have been quite effective, but there is no such approach
65   to sugar-laden products. Even so, the city of San Francisco, California, recently instituted a ban on including toys with unhealthy meals such as some types of fast food. A limit — or, ideally, ban — on television commercials for products with added sugars could further protect children's health. ...
70   Ultimately, food producers and distributors must reduce the amount of sugar added to foods. But sugar is cheap, sugar tastes good, and sugar sells, so companies have little incentive to change. Although one institution alone can't turn this juggernaut[5] around, the US Food and Drug Administration could "set the table" for change. To start, it should
75   consider removing fructose from the Generally Regarded as Safe (GRAS) list, which allows food manufacturers to add unlimited amounts to any food. Opponents will argue that other nutrients on the GRAS list, such as iron and vitamins A and D, can also be toxic when over-consumed. However, unlike sugar, these substances have no abuse potential.
80   Removal from the GRAS list would send a powerful signal to the European Food Safety Authority and the rest of the world. ...

—Robert H. Lustig, Laura A. Schmidt, and Claire D. Brindis
excerpted and adapted from "The Toxic Truth About Sugar"
Nature, February 2, 2012

---

[5]juggernaut — powerful force

Text 4
Sugar Taxes Are Unfair and Unhealthy

If the regulatory discussion about sugar is going to be based on science, rather than science fiction, it needs to move beyond kicking the soda can.

Conventional wisdom says draconian[1] regulation—specifically, a
5   high tax—on sugary drinks and snacks reduces unhealthy consumption, and thereby improves public health. There are many reasons, however, why high sugar taxes are at best unsuccessful, and at worst economically and socially harmful.

Research finds that higher prices don't reduce soda consumption, for
10   example. No scientific studies demonstrate a difference either in aggregate[2] soda consumption or in child and adolescent Body Mass Index [BMI] between the two thirds of states with soda taxes and those without such taxes.

The study that did find taxes might lead to a moderate reduction in
15   soda consumption also found this had no effect on adolescent obesity, as the reduction was completely offset by increases in consumption of other calorific drinks.

Economic research finds sugar taxes are a futile instrument in influencing the behavior and habits of the overweight and the obese.

---

[1]draconian — severe
[2]aggregate — total

20   Why do sugar taxes fail? Those consumers who strongly prefer unhealthy foods continue to eat and drink according to their individual preferences until such time as it becomes prohibitively expensive to do so. Demand for food is largely insensitive to price. A 10 percent increase in price reduces consumption by less than 1 percent. Applied to soda, this
25   means that to reduce consumption by 10 percent, the tax rate on sugary drinks would need to be 100 percent!

A sugar tax also has undesirable social and economic consequences. This tax is economically regressive, as a disproportionate share of the tax is paid by low earners, who pay a higher proportion of their
30   incomes in sales tax and also consume a disproportionate share of sugary snacks and drinks.

Such taxes also have perverse, unintended consequences. Taxes on sugary snacks lead many consumers to replace the taxed food with equally unhealthy foods. Poorer consumers react to higher food prices
35   not by changing their diets but by consuming even fewer healthy foods, such as fruits and vegetables, and eating more processed foods. For instance, taxes levied specifically on sugar content increase saturated fat consumption.

Sugar taxes have failed where they've been tried, and are unfair and
40   unhealthy. Given that there's no compelling evidence they'll improve public health, we can't justify using the tax code to shape the sweetness of our dietary choices.   —Patrick Basham
excerpted and adapted from "Sugar Taxes Are Unfair and Unhealthy"
http://www.usnews.com, March 30, 2012

Part 3 —Text-Analysis Response

Your Task: Closely read the text provided on the following pages and write a well-developed, text-based response of two to three paragraphs. In your response, identify a central idea in the text and analyze how the author's use of one writing strategy (literary element or literary technique or rhetorical device) develops this central idea. Use strong and thorough evidence from the text to support your analysis. Do *not* simply summarize the text. You may use the margins to take notes as you read and scrap paper to plan your response. Write your response on a separate sheet of paper.

Guidelines:

Be sure to:
• Identify a central idea in the text
• Analyze how the author's use of *one* writing strategy (literary element or literary technique or rhetorical device) develops this central idea. Examples include: characterization, conflict, denotation/connotation, metaphor, simile, irony, language use, point-of-view, setting, structure, symbolism, theme, tone, etc.
• Use strong and thorough evidence from the text to support your analysis
• Organize your ideas in a cohesive and coherent manner
• Maintain a formal style of writing
• Follow the conventions of standard written English

Text

...In the air now, I feel a new excitement, a slight surge of energy, a new light of a new dawn. This anticipation is like grass in the path of a distant approaching thunderstorm. I feel that the "spirit line" out of our complacencies in art has been drawn. A fresh expression of
5   our passions, our joys and pains is in the making. A new generation of interpretations of our legends and stories, strengths and weaknesses as Navajo people are replacing the images of stoic[1] tribalism that so pervaded our recent art history. To paraphrase another artist, "realness instead of redness." I feel as do other young fine artists of the
10 northern reservation, that there is much potential for individual expression of beauty, of power, of mysteries to be created within the perimeter of our culture in this time. But what inspires us young Navajo artists to create these interpretations of our culture? What force drives us to seek fresher means of expression? We all have our reasons and means
15 to do this. It may be money, it may be recognition or self-satisfaction. For me, it is a means of confronting myself, my fears and mysteries. A means of coming to terms with childhood phobias and a recognition of my strength and weaknesses in this day. In Navajo society, it is necessary to journey that road to self-discovery. To attain a spiritual
20 growth, we will have to go beyond the world we retreat into. We must recognize and acknowledge this new high tech world, yet still maintain an identity. We must draw a line beyond which we don't venture. Be able to compromise wisely and know how much to expose of ourselves. Know ourselves and our past, yet still have faith in the
25 future. We are a segment of a society that has been thrust into the 20th century all within 30 years. We will not allow ourselves to become casualties in this collision of cultures. The art that we represent must be flexible and adaptable, like the nature of our grandfather, if it is to survive, lest we become brittle and blow away like shells of
30 dry piñon nuts. The art that we represent, like the role of the medicine man of today, must help in creating a positive evolution into this new era for our people and those coming after us. It will scream of tomorrow, yet be dressed in the truth of our past. I believe this to be a collective therapy for us, for our culture and our art. ...
35   When I was around four years old, I traveled with my grandmother to the foot of the Sacred Mountain of the West. During this time, she told me many things. She told me that we are responsible in maintaining and nurturing a good identity with our grandparents every single day. Each day before the sun rises, we should greet the new coming
40 day with pollen and re-affirm our relationship with it. To a young piñon tree, we greet *"Yá'áhtééh shima'sání"* (Hello, my grandmother); to a young juniper tree; *"Yá'áhtééh shí'cheii"* (hello, my grandfather).

---

[1]stoic — calm and uncomplaining

In this manner, we bring new light and life to our world. At this age
I learned to feel, see and smell my world. I still associate lots of pieces
45 of past experiences, painful and pleasant, to these subtleties. There are
few things more pleasant than waking up in the morning to see dew
on blades of grass, or to hear rolling of the thunder as dark clouds
gather on spring days. To smell wet sand and hear the raindrops
dancing on parched ground. The cornstalks weeping for joy. Forming
50 figures from clay and feeling like a god. The soft crunching sound in
the snow as I make my way home with a rabbit or two on moonlit
winters [*sic*] night, or even being momentarily lost in a blizzard.
To feel as a tumbleweed rolling across rough landscape, to see the
last ray of sunlight hitting the mesa after an autumn day, light reflecting
55 off a distant passing car makes me feel vulnerable and sad at times.
These past feelings and experiences, associated with time and places,
I regard as a reservoir of my inspiration.

Like most young Navajos my age, we spent many winter nights
gathered around our father, listening to stories passed down through
60 generations. We sat in expectation as we journeyed up from the womb
of the Mother in creation stories. We sat mesmerized by coyote stories.
Laughing at his antics and frightened by his cruelties. We sat in awe as
First Man and First Woman brought forth life upon the Fourth World.
We journey back from the west, the home of Changing Woman, into
65 the midst of the Four Sacred Mountains after the creation of our clans.
"Slayer of Enemies" and "Born for Water," the hero and savior of the
fourth world, came alive for us these nights. I felt the pain of their fathers'
testing in the roaring fire of the hearth. Their war with the Monster Gods
raged as the snow storm dusted outside our door, snow sifting through
70 the cracks of the door. Shadows leaping on cribbed wall of the
hooghan[2] brought to life the animal beings as the shoe game was
created. As the nights wore on, the youngest ones of us fell asleep where
we sat. My mother's spindle scratching the floor set the tempo of these
late night journeys…back.

75 From these sources I draw my inspirations. I am humbled by its
beauty and strengthened by its power. With great respect, I relive
this in every creation, every all-night Blessingway chant and every
vision of glory upon this land. With good intentions, I recreate this in
every piece of art: intentions of preserving and passing on, intentions
80 of sharing and inviting all good-willed people for the sake of us as
American Indians in general, as Navajos in particular and the beauty
of our culture. This culture through art, in whatever form, however
expressed, will endure. …

—Shonto W. Begay
excerpted from "The View From The Mesa: A Source of Navajo Creativty"
Anii Ánáádaalyaa'Ígíí (*Recent ones that are made*), 1988
Wheelright Museum of the American Indian

---

[2]hooghan — traditional dwelling of the Navajo people

January 2017
Part 1
Multiple-Choice Questions
Directions (1–24): Closely read each of the three passages below. After each passage, there are several multiple choice questions. Select the best suggested answer to each question and record your answer in the space provided. You may use the margins to take notes as you read.

Reading Comprehension Passage A

    …The windows were open and the room was filled with loud, unearthly shrieks. Mrs. Munson lived on the third floor, and across the street was a public school playground. In the late afternoon the noise was almost unbearable. God, if she'd only known about this before she signed the
5   lease! With a little grunt she closed both windows and as far as she was concerned they could stay that way for the next two years.
    But Mrs. Munson was far too excited to be really annoyed. Vini Rondo was coming to see her, imagine, Vini Rondo….and this very afternoon! When she thought about it she felt fluttering wings in her stomach. It
10 had been almost five years, and Vini had been in Europe all this time. Whenever Mrs. Munson found herself in a group discussing the war she invariably announced, "Well, you know I have a very dear friend in Paris this very minute, Vini Rondo, she was right there when the Germans marched in! I have positive nightmares when I think what she must be
15 going through!" Mrs. Munson said it as if it were she whose fate lay in the balance. …
    "Vini, back in America," she thought, never ceasing to revel in the wonder of it. She puffed up the small green pillows on the couch and sat down. With piercing eyes she examined her room. Funny you never really
20 see your surroundings until a visitor is expected. Well, Mrs. Munson sighed contentedly, that new girl had, for a rarity, restored pre-war standards.
    The door-bell rang abruptly. It buzzed twice before Mrs. Munson could move, she was that excited. Finally she composed herself and went
25 to answer.
    At first Mrs. Munson didn't recognize her. The woman who confronted her had no chic up-swept coiffure … indeed her hair hung rather limply and had an uncombed look. A print dress in January? Mrs. Munson tried to keep the disappointment out of her voice when she
30 said, "Vini, darling, I should have known you anywhere."
    The woman still stood in the threshold. Under her arm she carried a large pink box and her grey eyes looked out at Mrs. Munson curiously.
    "Would you, Bertha?" Her voice was a queer whisper. "That's nice, very nice. I should have recognized you, too, although you've gotten rather
35 fat. [sic] haven't you?" Then she accepted Mrs. Munson's extended hand and came in. …

Vini smiled and Mrs. Munson noticed how irregular her teeth were and decided they could do with a good brushing.

"So," Vini continued, "when I got back in New York last week I
40 thought of you at once. I had an awful time trying to find you because I couldn't remember your husband's first name...."

"Albert," Mrs. Munson put in unnecessarily.

"... but I finally did and here I am. You know, Bertha, I really started thinking about you when I decided to get rid of my mink coat."
45   Mrs. Munson saw a sudden blush on Vini's face.

"Your mink coat?"

"Yes," Vini said, lifting up the pink box. "You remember my mink coat. You always admired it so. You always said it was the loveliest coat you'd ever seen." She started to undo the frayed silk ribbon that held the
50 box together.

"Of course, yes of course," Mrs. Munson said, letting the "course" trill down softly.

"I said to myself, 'Vini Rondo, what on earth do you need that coat for? Why not let Bertha have it?' You see, Bertha, I bought the most
55 gorgeous sable in Paris and you can understand that I really don't need two fur coats. Besides I have my silver-fox jacket."

Mrs. Munson watched her parting the tissue paper in the box, saw the chipped enamel on her nails, saw that her fingers were jewel-less, and suddenly realized a great many other things.
60   "So I thought of you and unless you want it I'll just keep it because I couldn't bear to think of anyone else having it." She held the coat and stood turning it this way and that. It was a beautiful coat; the fur shone rich and very smooth. Mrs. Munson reached out and ran her fingers across it ruffling the tiny hairs the wrong way.
65 Without thinking she said: "How much?"

Mrs. Munson brought back her hand quickly, as though she had touched fire, and then she heard Vini's voice, small and tired.

"I paid almost a thousand for it. Is a thousand too much?"

Down in the street Mrs. Munson could hear the deafening roar of
70 the playground and for once she was grateful. It gave her something else to concentrate on, something to lessen the intensity of her own feelings.

"I'm afraid that's too much. I really can't afford it," Mrs. Munson said distractedly, still staring at the coat, afraid to lift her eyes and see the other woman's face.
75   Vini tossed the coat on the couch. "Well, I want you to have it. It's not so much the money, but I feel I should get something back on my investment....How much could you afford?"

Mrs. Munson closed her eyes. Oh, God, this was awful! Just plain damned awful!
80   "Maybe four hundred," she answered weakly. ...

Vini leaned against the wall, her pale face looking hard in the magnified sunlight of the big bedroom windows.

"You can make out the check to me," she said disinterestedly.

"Yes, of course," Mrs. Munson said, suddenly coming back to earth.
85 Imagine Bertha Munson with a mink of her own!

They went back into the livingroom and she wrote the check for Vini. Carefully folding it, Vini deposited it in her small beaded purse.

Mrs. Munson tried hard to make conversation but she came up against a cold wall at each new channel. Once she asked, "Where is your husband,
90 Vini? You must bring him around for Albert to talk to." And Vini answered, "Oh, him! I haven't seen him for aeons. He's still in Lisbon for all I know." And so that was that.

Finally, after promising to phone the next day, Vini left. When she had gone Mrs. Munson thought, "Why, poor Vini, she's nothing but
95 a refugee!" Then she took her new coat and went into the bedroom. She couldn't tell Albert how she got it, that was definite. My, but he would be mad about the money! She decided to hide it in the furthest reaches of her closet and then one day she'd bring it out and say, "Albert look at the divine mink I bought at an auction. I got it for next to nothing."
100 Groping in the darkness of her closet she caught the coat on a hook. She gave a little yank and was terrified to hear the sound of ripping. Quickly she snapped on the light and saw that the sleeve was torn. She held the tear apart and pulled slightly. It ripped more and then some more. With a sick emptiness she knew the whole thing was rotten.
105 "Oh, my God [*sic*] she said, clutching at the linen rose in her hair, "Oh, my God, I've been taken and taken good, and there's nothing in the world I can do about it, nothing in the world!" For suddenly Mrs. Munson realized Vini wouldn't phone tomorrow or ever again.

—Truman Capote
excerpted from "A Mink of One's Own"
Decade of Short Stories, 1944

1.   The opening paragraph introduces Mrs. Munson's character by establishing her
(1) compassion   (3) intolerance
(2) deception   (4) resourcefulness   1 ____

2.   The statement "Mrs. Munson said it as if it were she whose fate lay in the balance" (lines 15 and 16) serves to illustrate Mrs. Munson's desire to
(1) impress others   (3) justify behavior
(2) incite conflicts   (4) avoid criticism   2 ____

3.   Lines 26 through 30 signal a transition in Mrs. Munson's attitude from one of
(1) loyalty to betrayal   (3) friendship to hostility
(2) anticipation to confusion (4) sympathy to indifference 3 ____

4. The description in line 45 implies that Vini has a
(1) carefree past   (3) fiery temper
(2) hidden motive   (4) secret identity   4 ____

5. The purpose of Vini's comments in lines 53 through 56 is to
(1) expose Vini's stinginess   (3) characterize Mrs. Munson
(2) describe Vini's coat   (4) entrap Mrs. Munson   5 ____

6. Based on the details in lines 57 through 59, Mrs. Munson
discovers that Vini
(1) is meticulous about her appearance
(2) is comfortable in her circumstances
(3) has an inflated self-image
(4) has experienced difficult times   6 ____

7. Lines 83 through 85 refine a central idea by emphasizing Mrs. Munson's
(1) indignation regarding Vini   (3) concern for appearances
(2) irritation with negotiators   (4) suspicion regarding Vini   7 ____

8. In the context of the text as a whole, the purpose of Mrs. Munson's
imagined conversation in lines 98 and 99 is to
(1) convince her husband to buy her a new mink
(2) rehearse an excuse for a costly purchase
(3) protect an acquaintance from persecution
(4) share her successful negotiations with her husband   8 ____

9. What mood is created by the final paragraph?
(1) desperation   (2) aggression   (3) satisfaction   (4) exhilaration   9 ____

10. Which statement from the text best foreshadows Vini Rondo's
true intentions for the visit?
(1) "Funny you never really see your surroundings until a visitor
is expected." (lines 19 and 20)
(2) "It buzzed twice before Mrs. Munson could move, she was
that excited." (lines 23 and 24)
(3) "The woman who confronted her had no chic up-swept
coiffure … indeed her hair hung rather limply and had an
uncombed look." (lines 26 through 28)
(4) "Down in the street Mrs. Munson could hear the deafening
roar of the playground and for once she was grateful."
(lines 69 and 70)   10 ____

Reading Comprehension Passage B
In the Wild

My brother and I hardly talk. I talk to my lawn mower
more and I don't have a lawn mower. I have a lawn
that's mostly clover and spots where dirt
has refused clover. The clover comes over
5   from the fields surrounding my yard,
where cows graze and geese too, who drive the cows nuts
in how they are not cows. These territorial battles
are more familiar when they come with ties or guns.
I wish everyone who used a gun wore a tie
10   or everyone who wore a tie carried a surfboard.
If I surfed I could call my brother from the rolling,
sneering lip of the Pacific and ask how he's doing
in Alaska teaching kids whatever it is kids need to know,
how to solve for x, I guess. It would be one thing
15   were there one x and you solved the equation
and ever after wore the answer on your T-shirt
and life was keeping that T-shirt relatively clean,
but there are x xs to solve for and no one to say
this is the x that matters. This poem
20   needs a better attitude: things could be worse.
I could be an animal estranged[1] from its own kind
and mind by an awareness of its own kind
and mind and not the ocelot or giraffe
I suspect I am when I stay away from mirrors. Lately,
25   brother, I would so love to be the possum
that eats the dry cat food we leave out for gray cat
often and orange cat sometimes, the possum
who cleans himself—or herself, I'm not going to check—
very much like a cat. I'm not going to lie:
30   in the wild, we'd have gone our separate ways
long ago, and snarled if we met after that
had we the snarling apparatus, or run if our legs
were long and thin, or fought with tusks
or fangs, so what's wrong here: maybe nothing,
35   brother. And maybe every mute second is our last
last chance.

—Bob Hicok
from *The Georgia Review*
Winter 2010

---

[1]estranged — distant

11. The narrator's statements in lines 1 and 2 convey a sense of
(1) fear   (2) disbelief   (3) objectivity   (4) irony   11 ___

12. The reference to the T-shirt in lines 14 through 19 contributes
to a central idea by suggesting that
(1) errors are common   (3) stability is important
(2) relationships are complex   (4) desires are futile   12 ___

13. The figurative language in lines 19 and 20 serves to
(1) illustrate an example   (3) signal a transition
(2) foreshadow an event   (4) predict a resolution   13 ___

14. The language in lines 29 through 35 reveals the narrator's belief
that siblings are
(1) mutually dependent   (3) naturally oppositional
(2) generally friendly   (4) largely unconventional   14 ___

Reading Comprehension Passage C

Peter Lake lies deep in a maple forest near the Wisconsin-Michigan border. One day in July 2008 a group of scientists and graduate students led by ecologist Stephen Carpenter of the University of Wisconsin-Madison arrived at the lake with some fish. One by one, they dropped
5 12 largemouth bass into the water. Then they headed for home, leaving behind sensors that could measure water clarity every five minutes, 24 hours a day.

The scientists repeated the same trip two more times in 2009. Each time they dropped 15 more bass into the water. Months passed. The lake
10 cycled through the seasons. It froze over, thawed out and bloomed again with life. Then, in the summer of 2010, Peter Lake changed dramatically. Before the scientists started their experiment, the lake abounded in fathead minnows, pumpkinseeds and other small fish. Now, however, those once dominant predators were rare, for the most part eaten
15 by the largemouth bass. The few survivors hid in the shallows. Water fleas and other tiny animals that the small fish once devoured were now free to flourish. And because these diminutive animals graze on algae, the lake water became clearer. Two years later the ecosystem remains in its altered state.
20   Peter Lake's food web has flipped, shifting from a longstanding arrangement to a new one. Carpenter triggered the switchover on purpose, as part of an experiment he is running on the factors that lead to persistent changes in the mix of organisms eating and being eaten by one another. Yet in recent decades food webs across the world have
25 also been flipping, often unexpectedly, on a far greater scale. Jellyfish now dominate the waters off the coast of Namibia. Hungry snails and fungi are overrunning coastal marshes in North Carolina, causing them

to disintegrate. In the northwestern Atlantic, lobsters are proliferating
while cod have crashed.

30   Whether by fishing, converting land into farms and cities, or warming
the planet, humanity is putting tremendous stresses on the world's
ecosystems. As a result, ecologists expect many more food webs to flip
in the years ahead. Predicting those sudden changes is far from straight-
forward, however, because food webs can be staggeringly complex.

35   That is where Carpenter comes in. Taking advantage of 30 years of
ecological research at Peter Lake, Carpenter and his colleagues developed
mathematical models of ecological networks that allowed them to pick
up early-warning signs of the change that was coming, 15 months before
its food web flipped. "We could see it a good long ways in advance,"
40   Carpenter says.

With the help of such models, he and other scientists are beginning
to decipher some of the rules that determine whether a food web will
remain stable or cross a threshold and change substantially. They hope
to use their knowledge of those rules to monitor the state of ecosystems
45   so that they can identify ones at risk of collapse. Ideally, an early-warning
system would tell us when to alter human activities that are pushing an
ecosystem toward a breakdown or would even allow us to pull ecosystems
back from the brink. Prevention is key, they say, because once ecosystems
pass their tipping point, it is remarkably difficult for them to return.

Mathematical Predators

50   Carpenter's work builds on a century of basic research by ecologists
who have sought to answer a simple question: Why are the populations
of different species the way they are? Why, for example, are there so many
flies and so few wolves? And why do the sizes of fly populations vary
greatly from one year to the next? To find an answer, ecologists began to
55   diagram food webs, noting who ate whom and how much each one ate.
Yet food webs can encompass dozens, hundreds or thousands of species;
their complexity often turned attempted diagrams into hopeless snarls.

To make sense of the snarls, ecologists have turned food webs into
mathematical models. They write an equation for the growth of one species
60   by linking its reproduction rate to how much food it can obtain and how
often it gets eaten by other species. Because all those variables can change,
solving the equations for even simple food webs has proved overwhelming.
Fortunately, the rise of fast, cheap computers has recently allowed
ecologists to run simulations of many different kinds of ecosystems.

65   Out of this work, ecologists discovered some key principles operating
in real food webs. Most food webs, for instance, consist of many weak
links rather than a few strong ones. Two species are strongly linked if they
interact a lot, such as a predator that consistently devours huge numbers
of a single prey. Species that are weakly linked interact occasionally: a
70   predator snacks every now and then on various species. Food webs may
be dominated by numerous weak links because that arrangement is more

stable over the long term. If a predator can eat several species, it can survive the extinction of one of them. And if a predator can move on to another species that is easier to find when a prey species becomes rare, 75 the switch allows the original prey to recover. The weak links may thus keep species from driving one another to extinction. "You see it over and over again," says Kevin McCann, an ecologist at the University of Guelph in Ontario.

Mathematical models have also revealed vulnerable points in food 80 webs, where small changes can lead to big effects throughout entire ecosystems. In the 1960s, for example, theoreticians proposed that predators at the top of a food web exerted a surprising amount of control over the size of populations of other species—including species they did not directly attack. The idea of this top-down control by a small fraction 85 of animals in an ecosystem was greeted with skepticism. It was hard to see how a few top predators could have such a great effect on the rest of their food web.

But then we humans began running unplanned experiments that put this so-called trophic cascade[1] hypothesis to the test. In the ocean, we 90 fished for top predators such as cod on an industrial scale, while on land, we killed off large predators such as wolves. We introduced invasive species such as rats to islands and gave a variety of other shocks to the world's ecosystems. The results of these actions vindicated the key role of predators and the cascading effects they can have from the top of a 95 food web on down. ...

Carpenter is optimistic that the early-warning system he is developing will work not just in isolated lakes but in any ecosystem, thanks to the way ecological networks are organized. Yet success would not mean that predicting a flip would be certain. The equations that he and his colleagues 100 have developed suggest that some disturbances will be so dramatic and fast that they will not leave time for ecologists to notice that trouble is coming. "Surprises will continue," Carpenter says, "although the early-warning system does provide the opportunity to anticipate some surprises before they happen."

—Carl Zimmer
excerpted from "Ecosystems on the Brink"
Scientific American, October 2012

---

[1]trophic cascade — changes in the food chain caused by removal of the top predator

15. The first paragraph engages the reader by
—(1) describing an experiment without revealing its purpose
(2) challenging a theory and sharing the results
(3) citing data to disprove a theory
(4) introducing an issue to explain its implications   15 ___

16. As used in line 17, the word "diminutive" most nearly means
(1) unknown   —(2) little   (3) sickly   (4) solitary   16 ___

17. According to the author, the results of the Peter Lake experiment
(lines 20 through 24) were
—(1) intentional   (2) unethical   (3) exaggerated   (4) inconclusive   17 ___

18. The flipped food webs in Namibia, North Carolina, and the
Northwest Atlantic (lines 24 through 29) can best be characterized as
(1) artificial   (2) necessary   (3) planned   (4) problematic   18 ___

19. In lines 30 through 32, the author emphasizes that the main cause
for the flipping of food webs is
(1) emerging diseases   (3) natural disasters
—(2) human activity   (4) accelerated evolution   19 ___

20. According to lines 41 through 49, why is it important to predict
a possible change in an ecosystem?
(1) to expand human involvement
(2) to stop scientific experimentation
—(3) to forestall irreversible damage
(4) to identify potential benefits   20 ___

21. The author's use of questions in lines 51 through 54 establishes a
—(1) connection between population changes and scientific findings
(2) relationship between existing predators and prey populations
(3) dispute between prior research and experimental outcomes
(4) conflict between established theories and new ideas   21 ___

22. The author's use of the phrase "hopeless snarls" in line 52 connotes a
(1) savage nature   (3) distressed sound
(2) depressing situation   —(4) tangled mass   22 ___

23. The details presented in lines 65 through 75 help the reader to
understand the
(1) negative effects of weak links
(2) predators' need for one food source
—(3) importance of having multiple prey
(4) danger in natural flipping   23 ___

24. Which statement best summarizes a central idea of the text?
—(1) "Predicting those sudden changes is far from straightforward, however, because food webs can be staggeringly complex." (lines 33 and 34)
(2) "Fortunately, the rise of fast, cheap computers has recently allowed ecologists to run simulations of many different kinds of ecosystems." (lines 63 and 64)
(3) "Most food webs, for instance, consist of many weak links rather than a few strong ones." (lines 66 and 67)
(4) "But then we humans began running unplanned experiments that put this so-called trophic cascade hypothesis to the test." (lines 88 and 89)   24 ___

Part 2
Argument
Directions: Closely read each of the *four* texts provided on the following pages and write a source-based argument on the topic below. You may use the margins to take notes as you read and scrap paper to plan your response. Write your argument on a separate sheet of paper provided by the teacher.

Topic: Should the United States eliminate Daylight Saving Time?

Your Task: Carefully read each of the *four* texts provided. Then, using evidence from at least *three* of the texts, write a well-developed argument regarding whether or not the United States government should eliminate Daylight Saving Time. Clearly establish your claim, distinguish your claim from alternate or opposing claims, and use specific, relevant, and sufficient evidence from at least *three* of the texts to develop your argument. Do *not* simply summarize each text.

Guidelines:
Be sure to:
- Establish your claim regarding the elimination of Daylight Saving Time in the United States
- Distinguish your claim from alternate or opposing claims
- Use specific, relevant, and sufficient evidence from at least *three* of the texts to develop your argument
- Identify each source that you reference by text number and line number(s) or graphic (for example: Text 1, line 4 or Text 2, graphic)
- Organize your ideas in a cohesive and coherent manner
- Maintain a formal style of writing
- Follow the conventions of standard written English

Texts:
    Text 1 – History of Daylight Saving Time – DST
    Text 2 – Pros & Cons: Daylight Savings Time
    Text 3 – Seize the Daylight: The Curious and Contentious
                Story of Daylight Saving Time
    Text 4 – The Cost of Daylight Saving Time

Text 1
History of Daylight Saving Time – DST

DST is a change in the standard time with the purpose of making better use of daylight and conserving energy.

Clocks are set ahead one hour when DST starts. This means that the sunrise and sunset will be one hour later, on the clock, than the day before.

5   Although DST has only been used for about 100 years, the idea was conceived many years before. Ancient civilizations are known to have engaged in a practice similar to modern DST where they would adjust their daily schedules to the Sun's schedule. For example, the Roman water clocks used different scales for different months of the Year. ...

10   Germany was the first country to implement DST. Clocks there were first turned forward at 11:00 p.m. (23:00[1]) on April 30, 1916.

The rationale was to minimize the use of artificial lighting in order to save fuel for the war effort during World War I. The idea was quickly followed by Britain and many other countries, including the United States. Many

15   countries reverted back to standard time post-World War I. It wasn't until the next World War that DST made its return in many countries in order to save vital energy resources for the war. ...

In the United States, DST caused widespread confusion from 1945 to 1966 for trains, buses and the broadcasting industry because states and

20   localities were free to choose when and if they would observe DST. Congress decided to end the confusion and establish the Uniform Time Act of 1966 that stated DST would begin on the last Sunday of April and end on the last Sunday of October. However, states still had the ability to be exempt from DST by passing a local ordinance.

25   The U.S. Congress extended DST to a period of ten months in 1974 and eight months in 1975, in hopes to save energy following the 1973 oil embargo. The trial period showed that DST saved the energy equivalent of 10,000 barrels of oil each day, but DST still proved to be controversial. Many complained that the dark winter mornings endangered the lives of children

30   going to school. After the energy crisis was over in 1976, the U.S. changed their DST schedule again to begin on the last Sunday in April. DST was amended again to begin on the first Sunday in April 1987. Further changes were made after the introduction of the *Energy Policy Act of 2005*. ...

The DST schedule in the U.S. was revised several times throughout the

35   years. From 1987 to 2006, the country observed DST for about seven months each year. The current schedule was introduced in 2007 and follows the Energy Policy Act of 2005, which extended the period by about one month. Today, DST starts on the second Sunday in March and ends on the first Sunday in November. Currently, most of the United States observes DST

40   except for Hawaii and most of Arizona, as well as the U.S. insular areas of Puerto Rico, the U.S. Virgin Islands, American Samoa, and Guam.

—excerpted from "History of Daylight Saving Time – DST"
timeanddate.com, 1995-2014

---

[1]23:00 — military time

Text 2
Pros & Cons: Daylight Savings Time

What are the Pros of "Daylight Savings Time"?...

Reduces Exposure to Artificial Lighting

An advantage of daylight savings time is the ability to reduce exposure to artificial lighting, which is the use of lamps and light fixtures. It is valuable to provide the correct light intensity and color spectrum for each task or environment. Otherwise, energy not only could be wasted but over-
5 illumination can lead to adverse health and psychological effects. Beyond the energy factors being considered, it is important not to over-design illumination, lest adverse health effects such as headache frequency, stress, and increased blood pressure be induced by the higher lighting levels. In addition, glare or excess light can decrease worker efficiency. ...

Prevents Vitamin D Deficiency

10 An advantage of observing daylight savings time is having the ability to prevent vitamin D deficiency that is produced by the body from sunlight. Excessive seclusion from the sun may lead to vitamin D deficiency unless adequate amounts are obtained through diet. A lack of sunlight, on the other hand, is considered one of the primary causes of Seasonal Affective Disorder
15 (SAD), a serious form of the "winter blues". SAD occurrence is more prevalent in locations farther from the tropics, and most of the treatments (other than prescription drugs) involve light therapy, replicating sunlight through lamps tuned to specific wavelengths of visible light, or full-spectrum bulbs. According to a study conducted by the American Academy of Neurology,
20 results indicate that more exposure to sunshine early in a person's life relates to less risk from Multiple Sclerosis (MS) later in life.

Increases Sunlight Effect on Cardiovascular Illnesses

An advantage of observing daylight savings time is the effect on cardiovascular illnesses through having additional sunlight exposure from the shift in time. In January 2014, British researchers found that sunlight may
25 lower blood pressure, a dangerous factor for heart attacks and stroke. It was reported that 20 minutes of Ultraviolet A (UVA) sunlight lowered blood pressure by a small but significant amount by dilating[1] blood vessels and easing hypertension.[2] The Journal of Investigative Dermatology[3] tested 24 volunteers and found that the sun increases nitric oxide levels, a chemical
30 linked to blood flow, and results in lowered blood pressure. This research supports the claim of Richard Weller of the University of Edinburgh and Martin Feelisch of the University of Southampton, who found that people who live in the darker north have higher rates of heart disease. They concluded, "We are concerned that well-meaning advice to reduce the comparatively low
35 numbers of deaths from skin cancer may inadvertently increase the risk of death from far higher prevalent cardiovascular disease and stroke, and goes

---

[1]dilating — enlarging

[2]hypertension — high blood pressure

[3]dermatology — branch of medical science dealing with the skin and its diseases

against epidemiological[4] data showing that sunlight exposure reduces all cause and cardiovascular mortality."... What are the Cons of "Daylight Savings Time"?...

Effects Health & Healthcare Devices

40   A disadvantage of observing daylight savings time is the effects on health and healthcare devices, especially when adequately not prepared in advance for the time change. Some experience sleep deprivation and poor health due to the shift in time during the implementation of daylight savings time. Medical devices may generate adverse events that could harm patients, without being
45 obvious to clinicians responsible for care. These problems are compounded when the daylight savings time rules themselves change; software developers must test and perhaps modify many programs, and users must install updates and restart applications. Consumers must update devices such as programmable thermostats or manually adjust the devices' clocks. Medical devices, such
50 as pacemakers, defibrillators, and glucose monitors, have to be adjusted as serious consequences may result if ignored since these devices operate on a standard schedule. Some studies have also found that more heart attacks tend to occur after the shift in time as well as the increase in suicide rates. ...

Disturbs Sleep Pattern

A disadvantage of observing daylight savings time is the disturbance in
55 sleep pattern, especially for those that are critical of time punctuality. Light plays an integral role in sleep, in which light suppresses the secretion of the sleep-inducing substance melatonin. Light exposure tends to advance the circadian rhythm that is crucial during waking stage while darkness impedes the circadian rhythm which is crucial for sleeping. Those exposed to
60 significant amounts of light directly before sleep are claimed by several surveys to have [sic] harder time waking up. Thus, the shift in time is likely to disturb sleep patterns to various extents that differs between individuals in accordance of each individuals [sic] personal sleep behaviors. ...

Effects Farmers' Morning Productivity

A disadvantage of observing daylight savings time is the effects
65 experienced on farmers' morning productivity. Farmers oppose daylight savings time on the basis that grain is best harvested after dew evaporates, so when field hands arrive and leave earlier in summer their labor is less valuable. For such farmers, daylight earlier in the day is more beneficial rather than in the evening. Dairy farmers are another group that complains
70 of time change as their cows are sensitive to the timing of milking, so when their deliveries need to be made earlier their systems are disrupted. Conclusively, observing daylight savings time is a disadvantage for farmers that are highly dependent on a consistent time schedule which can deter their production. ...

—excerpted from "Pros & Cons: Daylight Savings Time"
theprocons.com, October 22, 2014

---

[4]epidemiological — factors controlling the presence or absence of disease

Text 3
Seize the Daylight: The Curious and Contentious[1] Story of Daylight Saving Time

... A primary impact of daylight saving time is the reduction of energy consumption, and this has been the major impetus[2] for numerous countries to adopt DST. Because factories, businesses, and government offices, among others, often open at a time when the sun has already risen but do not close
5   until after sunset, a clock advance of one hour allows them to save significant energy for lighting. The extra hour of evening daylight saves most households one hour of electricity for evening lighting, and also draws people outdoors, cutting additional indoor energy use. This savings may be wholly or partially offset by additional lighting needed in the morning, but many people sleep
10   through the hour of sunrise, whereas almost everyone is awake during the hour of sunset. DST also often reduces the daily peak needed for electricity production (when the least efficient power sources are used) by spreading out usage to later in the evening. The DOT [Department of Transportation] concluded that the total electricity savings associated with DST amounted
15   to about 1 percent in spring and fall, corresponding to national savings of forty to fifty megawatt hours per day.

     DST also might affect home heating, air conditioning, and other forms of energy consumption. For example, the extra hour of light in the evening could cause an increase in recreational and shopping travel by automobile
20   (and therefore an increase in gasoline consumption) that might not be offset by a corresponding decrease in the morning. On the other hand, more outdoor activities might save energy by decreasing the use of TV sets and appliances. The DOT did not detect any significant DST impact on these areas.

     Another major impact of DST is the reduction of motor-vehicle accidents
25   and fatalities. Driving after dark is much more dangerous than driving in daylight, and while there are other factors, this difference results primarily from decreased visibility. Since DST makes evenings lighter and mornings darker, the evening accident rate should decrease, while the morning rate should increase, for drivers and passengers as well as pedestrians. Since
30   evenings see significantly more traffic than mornings — often twice as much — the overall daily accidents might be expected to decrease under DST. And better visibility is all the more important when another element is considered: early-evening drivers are more likely than morning drivers to be tired or inebriated.[3] Certainly, traffic-pattern changes, weather, and other
35   factors also may play a role in the incidence of accidents, but a shift to DST would be expected to reduce total accidents. In fact, the DOT study found a 0.7 percent decrease in fatal motor vehicle accidents for March and April under DST as compared with standard time. The decline was small but important, corresponding to approximately fifty lives saved and two thousand
40   injuries avoided for the two-month period.

---

[1]contentious — controversial
[2]impetus — cause
[3]inebriated — intoxicated

On the heated topic of safety for schoolchildren, dark DST mornings increase the risk of accidents for children on their way to school. However, the extra light from DST in the late afternoon decreases the risk of accidents for children in activities such as riding bicycles, engaging in unsupervised
45   outdoor play, or traveling as passengers in cars. The DOT study found that under DST in March and April, the increase in morning accidents seemed to be more than offset by the decrease in evening accidents. Despite these findings, one political fact was crystal clear: The news stories of the tragic deaths of young victims in morning accidents carried far more emotional
50   weight than statistics showing that fatalities were avoided in the evening.
        Another area of DST impact is crime reduction. People generally feel safer in the daylight, and many types of crime are believed to be influenced by lighting conditions. For example, more light in the evening decreases the opportunity for street crime against people returning home from work.
55   The DOT study found that violent crime in Washington, D.C., was reduced by 10 to 13 percent during periods of daylight saving time. ...
        Daylight saving time benefits many enterprises related to outdoor pursuits, and it also impacts a number of other economic areas, such as manufacturing, domestic trade, construction and public transportation. Groups
60   surveyed in these areas mildly favored DST or felt it had no effect. A shift of clock time under DST lengthens the overlap of U.S. business hours with Europe and shortens the overlap with Japan. A DOT analysis showed no DST effect on communications with Japan, but an increase in communications with Europe. ...

—David Prerau
excerpted and adapted from *Seize the Daylight: The Curious and Contentious Story of Daylight Saving Time*, 2005
Thunder's Mouth Press

Text 4
The Cost of Daylight Saving Time

... It turns out that more daylight gives us more time to shop, drive, grill and perfect our golf game. What it doesn't do is cut our energy use, as is the intent, says Michael Downing, a lecturer in English and author of Spring Forward: *The Annual Madness of Daylight Saving Time.*
5   In fact, when we lose an hour's sleep at 2 a.m. on March 9 [2014] —beginning the eight month DST season—it will not reduce our electricity use even by one half of 1 percent, says Downing, contrary to the most recent study by the Department of Energy.
        While the government continues to claim that the country reduces
10   electricity use for each day during DST, Downing says we come nowhere near that. Some studies do report small reductions in electricity use, but the most comprehensive study of household energy demand and many others report an increase in overall energy consumption ranging from 1 to 4 percent during DST.

15   "The barbeque grill and charcoal industries say they gain $200 million in sales with an extra month of daylight saving—and they were among the biggest lobbies in favor of extending DST from six to seven months in 1986," he says. Lobbying alongside them that year was the golf industry, which says that additional month of daylight has meant more time on the

20   links and an additional $400 million in revenue.

    But what's good for retail is bad for overall energy use, says Downing. "If it's light when we leave work and we decide to go to the mall or a restaurant or head for a summer night at the beach, we don't walk there; we get in our cars," he says.

25   Gas consumption goes up during daylight saving time—"something the gas industry has known since the 1930s," Downing says. That's why it lobbied hard to reintroduce DST after two short-term experiments with it to conserve electricity and other energy resources during World Wars I and II.

    But more driving also means more carbon dioxide in the atmosphere,

30   which exacerbates[1] climate change, says Downing. Moreover, the reduced cost of indoor lighting on sunny spring and summer afternoons is offset by higher air-conditioning costs at offices, factories and shopping malls.

    "Every time the government studies [DST], it turns out that we are really saving nothing when all is said and done," Downing says.

35   And yet, at the urging of many industry lobbies, the government has extended the duration of DST several times. In 1966, President Lyndon B. Johnson signed the Uniform Time Act, which instituted daylight saving time, beginning on the last Sunday of April and ending the last Sunday of October —six months in all. This act standardized customs that varied from state to

40   state between 1945 and 1966.

    Then in 1986, the federal law was amended to add a full month to DST, making it begin the first, not the last, Sunday in April. "This change was spurred by a large number of lobbies: golf and golf equipment, home improvement, the Hearth, Patio and Barbecue Association and the gas and

45   fuel industries, which saw a potential boon to their sales," Downing says. "There was little concern for those living in western parts of each time zone, where sunrise could be as late as 8:30 a.m. some months. ...

    In 2005, seven months of DST became eight with the passage of the Energy Policy Act, which moved the start date to the second Sunday of

50   March and ended it a week later, on the first Sunday in November. The change from the end of October to early November was not driven by energy savings, but by the National Association of Convenience Stores (NACS), who wanted Halloween to occur during DST. ...

    "So today we have eight months of daylight saving and only four months

55   of standard time," he says. "Can you tell me which time is the standard?" ...

—Gail Bambrick
excerpted and adapted from "The Cost of Daylight Saving Time"
now.tufts.edu, March 4, 2014

---

[1]exacerbates — aggravates

Part 3
Text-Analysis Response

Your Task: Closely read the following text provided and write a well-developed, text-based response of two to three paragraphs. In your response, identify a central idea in the text and analyze how the author's use of *one* writing strategy (literary element or literary technique or rhetorical device) develops this central idea. Use strong and thorough evidence from the text to support your analysis. Do not simply summarize the text. You may use the margins to take notes as you read and scrap paper to plan your response. Write your response on a separate sheet of paper.

Guidelines:

   Be sure to:
- Identify a central idea in the text
- Analyze how the author's use of *one* writing strategy (literary element or literary technique or rhetorical device) develops this central idea. Examples include: characterization, conflict, denotation/connotation, metaphor, simile, irony, language use, point-of-view, setting, structure, symbolism, theme, tone, etc.
- Use strong and thorough evidence from the text to support your analysis
- Organize your ideas in a cohesive and coherent manner
- Maintain a formal style of writing
- Follow the conventions of standard written English

Text 1

    He came into the room to shut the windows while we were still in bed and I saw he looked ill. He was shivering, his face was white, and he walked slowly as though it ached to move.

    "What's the matter, Schatz?"

5   "I've got a headache."

    "You better go back to bed."

    "No. I'm all right."

    "You go to bed. I'll see you when I'm dressed."

    But when I came downstairs he was dressed, sitting by the fire, looking

10 a very sick and miserable boy of nine years. When I put my hand on his forehead I knew he had a fever.

    "You go up to bed," I said, "you're sick."

    "I'm all right," he said.

    When the doctor came he took the boy's temperature.

15   "What is it?" I asked him.

    "One hundred and two."

    Downstairs, the doctor left three different medicines in different colored capsules with instructions for giving them. One was to bring down the fever, another a purgative,[1] the third to overcome an acid condition. The germs

---
[1] purgative — laxative

20 of influenza can only exist in an acid condition, he explained. He seemed to
know all about influenza and said there was nothing to worry about if the fever
did not go above one hundred and four degrees. This was a light epidemic
of flu and there was no danger if you avoided pneumonia.

Back in the room I wrote the boy's temperature down and made a note
25 of the time to give the various capsules.

"Do you want me to read to you?"

"All right. If you want to," said the boy. His face was very white and
there were dark areas under his eyes. He lay still in the bed and seemed very
detached from what was going on.

30   I read aloud from Howard Pyle's *Book of Pirates*; but I could see he
was not following what I was reading.

"How do you feel, Schatz?" I asked him.

"Just the same, so far," he said.

I sat at the foot of the bed and read to myself while I waited for it to be
35 time to give another capsule. It would have been natural for him to go to
sleep, but when I looked up he was looking at the foot of the bed, looking very
strangely.

"Why don't you try to go to sleep? I'll wake you up for the medicine."

"I'd rather stay awake."

40   After a while he said to me, "You don't have to stay in here with me, Papa,
if it bothers you."

"It doesn't bother me."

"No, I mean you don't have to stay if it's going to bother you."

I thought perhaps he was a little lightheaded and after giving him the
45 prescribed capsules at eleven o'clock I went out for a while. It was a bright,
cold day, the ground covered with a sleet that had frozen so that it seemed as
if all the bare trees, the bushes, the cut brush and all the grass and the bare
ground had been varnished with ice. I took the young Irish setter for a
little walk up the road and along a frozen creek, but it was difficult to stand
50   or walk on the glassy surface and the red dog slipped and slithered and I
fell twice, hard, once dropping my gun and having it slide away over the ice.

We flushed a covey[2] of quail under a high clay bank with overhanging
brush and I killed two as they went out of sight over the top of the bank. Some
of the covey lit in trees, but most of them scattered into brush piles and it
55 was necessary to jump on the ice-coated mounds of brush several times
before they would flush. Coming out while you were poised unsteadily on
the icy, springy brush they made difficult shooting and I killed two, missed
five, and started back pleased to have found a covey close to the house and
happy there were so many left to find on another day.

60   At the house they said the boy had refused to let any one come into the
room.

"You can't come in," he said. "You mustn't get what I have."

---

[2]covey — flock

I went up to him and found him in exactly the position I had left him, white-faced, but with the tops of his cheeks flushed by the fever, staring still, as he had stared, at the foot of the bed.

I took his temperature.

"What is it?"

"Something like a hundred," I said. It was one hundred and two and four tenths.

"It was a hundred and two," he said.

"Who said so?"

"The doctor."

"Your temperature is all right," I said. "It's nothing to worry about."

"I don't worry," he said, "but I can't keep from thinking."

"Don't think," I said. "Just take it easy."

"I'm taking it easy," he said and looked straight ahead. He was evidently holding tight onto himself about something.

"Take this with water."

"Do you think it will do any good?"

"Of course it will."

I sat down and opened the *Pirate* book and commenced to read, but I could see he was not following, so I stopped.

"About what time do you think I'm going to die?" he asked.

"What?"

"About how long will it be before I die?"

"You aren't going to die. What's the matter with you?"

"Oh, yes, I am. I heard him say a hundred and two."

"People don't die with a fever of one hundred and two. That's a silly way to talk."

"I know they do. At school in France the boys told me you can't live with forty-four degrees. I've got a hundred and two."

He had been waiting to die all day, ever since nine o'clock in the morning.

"You poor Schatz," I said. "Poor old Schatz. It's like miles and kilometers. You aren't going to die. That's a different thermometer. On that thermometer thirty-seven is normal. On this kind it's ninety-eight."

"Are you sure?"

"Absolutely," I said. "It's like miles and kilometers. You know, like how many kilometers we make when we do seventy miles in the car?"

"Oh," he said.

But his gaze at the foot of the bed relaxed slowly. The hold over himself relaxed too, finally, and the next day it was very slack and he cried very easily at little things that were of no importance.

—Ernest Hemingway
"A Day's Wait"
Winner Take Nothing, 1933
Charles Scribner's Sons

June 2017
Part 1
Multiple-Choice Questions

Directions (1–24): Closely read each of the three passages below. After each passage, there are several multiple choice questions. Select the best suggested answer to each question and record your answer in the space provided. You may use the margins to take notes as you read.

Reading Comprehension Passage A

    I received one morning a letter, written in pale ink on glassy, blue-lined note-paper, and bearing the postmark of a little Nebraska village. This communication, worn and rubbed, looking as if it had been carried for some days in a coat pocket that was none too clean, was from my uncle
5 Howard, and informed me that his wife had been left a small legacy by a bachelor relative, and that it would be necessary for her to go to Boston to attend to the settling of the estate. He requested me to meet her at the station and render her whatever services might be necessary. On examining the date indicated as that of her arrival, I found it to be no later
10 than tomorrow. He had characteristically delayed writing until, had I been . away from home for a day, I must have missed my aunt altogether. ...
    Whatever shock Mrs. Springer [the landlady] experienced at my aunt's appearance, she considerately concealed. As for myself, I saw my aunt's battered figure with that feeling of awe and respect with which we
15 behold explorers who have left their ears and fingers north of Franz-Joseph-Land,[1] or their health somewhere along the Upper Congo. My Aunt Georgiana had been a music teacher at the Boston Conservatory, somewhere back in the latter sixties [1860s]. One summer, while visiting in the little village among the Green Mountains where her ancestors had
20 dwelt for generations, she had kindled the callow[2] fancy of my uncle, Howard Carpenter, then an idle, shiftless boy of twenty-one. When she returned to her duties in Boston, Howard followed her, and the upshot of this infatuation was that she eloped with him, eluding the reproaches of her family and the criticism of her friends by going with him to the
25 Nebraska frontier. Carpenter, who, of course, had no money, took up a homestead in Red Willow County, fifty miles from the railroad. There they had measured off their land themselves, driving across the prairie in a wagon, to the wheel of which they had tied a red cotton handkerchief, and counting its revolutions. They built a dug-out in the red hillside,
30 one of those cave dwellings whose inmates so often reverted to primitive conditions. Their water they got from the lagoons where the buffalo drank, and their slender stock of provisions was always at the mercy of bands of roving Indians. For thirty years my aunt had not been farther than fifty miles from the homestead.

---

[1]Franz-Joseph-Land — Russian archipelago of 191 islands in the Arctic Ocean
[2]callow — naive

35   I owed to this woman most of the good that ever came my way in my boyhood, and had a reverential[3] affection for her. During the years when I was riding herd for my uncle, my aunt, after cooking the three meals — the first of which was ready at six o'clock in the morning — and putting the six children to bed, would often stand until midnight at
40 her ironing-board, with me at the kitchen table beside her, hearing me recite Latin declensions and conjugations, gently shaking me when my drowsy head sank down over a page of irregular verbs. It was to her, at her ironing or mending, that I read my first Shakspere, and her old text-book on mythology was the first that ever came into my empty hands.
45 She taught me my scales and exercises on the little parlour organ which her husband had bought her after fifteen years during which she had not so much as seen a musical instrument. She would sit beside me by the hour, darning and counting, while I struggled with the "Joyous Farmer." She seldom talked to me about music, and I understood why. Once when
50 I had been doggedly beating out some easy passages from an old score of *Euryanthe* I had found among her music books, she came up to me and, putting her hands over my eyes, gently drew my head back upon her shoulder, saying tremulously, "Don't love it so well, Clark, or it may be taken from you."…
55   At two o'clock the Symphony Orchestra was to give a Wagner program, and I intended to take my aunt; though, as I conversed with her, I grew doubtful about her enjoyment of it. I suggested our visiting the Conservatory and the Common before lunch, but she seemed altogether too timid to wish to venture out. She questioned me absently about
60 various changes in the city, but she was chiefly concerned that she had forgotten to leave instructions about feeding half-skimmed milk to a certain weakling calf, "old Maggie's calf, you know, Clark," she explained, evidently having forgotten how long I had been away. She was further troubled because she had neglected to tell her daughter about the freshly-
65 opened kit of mackerel[4] in the cellar, which would spoil if it were not used directly. …

     The first number [of the concert] was the *Tannhauser*[5] overture. When the horns drew out the first strain of the Pilgrim's chorus, Aunt Georgiana clutched my coat sleeve. Then it was I first realized that for her this broke
70 a silence of thirty years. With the battle between the two motives,[6] with the frenzy of the Venusberg theme and its ripping of strings, there came to me an overwhelming sense of the waste and wear we are so powerless to combat; and I saw again the tall, naked house on the prairie, black and grim as a wooden fortress; the black pond where I had learned to swim,
75 its margin pitted with sun-dried cattle tracks; the rain gullied clay banks

---

[3]reverential — with great honor and respect
[4]kit of mackerel — container of fish
[5]*Tannhauser* — an opera by Richard Wagner
[6]motives — recurrent musical phrases

about the naked house, the four dwarf ash seedlings where the dish-cloths were always hung to dry before the kitchen door. The world there was the flat world of the ancients; to the east, a cornfield that stretched to daybreak; to the west, a corral that reached to sunset; between, the
80 conquests of peace, dearer-bought than those of war. ...

Her lip quivered and she hastily put her handkerchief up to her mouth. From behind it she murmured, "And you have been hearing this ever since you left me, Clark?" Her question was the gentlest and saddest of reproaches. ...

85   The deluge of sound poured on and on; I never knew what she found in the shining current of it; I never knew how far it bore her, or past what happy islands. From the trembling of her face I could well believe that before the last number she had been carried out where the myriad graves are, into the grey, nameless burying grounds of the sea; or into some world
90 of death vaster yet, where, from the beginning of the world, hope has lain down with hope and dream with dream and, renouncing, slept. ...

I spoke to my aunt. She burst into tears and sobbed pleadingly. "I don't want to go, Clark, I don't want to go!"

I understood. For her, just outside the concert hall, lay the black pond
95 with the cattle-tracked bluffs; the tall, unpainted house, with weather-curled boards, naked as a tower; the crook-backed ash seedlings where the dish-cloths hung to dry; the gaunt, moulting turkeys picking up refuse about the kitchen door.

—Willa Cather excerpted and adapted from "A Wagner Matinée"
Youth and the Bright Medusa, April 1920

1.   A primary function of the first paragraph is to
(1) establish the reason for the meeting
(2) create an atmosphere of mystery
(3) identify preferences of the narrator's aunt
(4) reveal flaws in the narrator's character   1 ____

2.   In lines 1 through 11, the commentary about the letter implies that the narrator believes his uncle is
(1) uncomfortable with changes   (3) angry with his wife
(2) careless about details   (4) disappointed at his decision   2 ____

3.   The details in lines 16 through 25 suggest that in her youth Aunt Georgiana was
(1) courageous yet hesitant   (3) resourceful yet cautious
(2) compassionate yet critical   (4) intelligent yet impulsive   3 ____

4.   Lines 33 and 34, "For thirty years my aunt had not been farther than fifty miles from the homestead" reinforces a sense of
(1) discomfort   (2) happiness   (3) isolation   (4) affection   4 ____

5.   Which statement from the passage best explains the narrator's "reverential affection" (line 36) for his Aunt Georgiana?
(1) "It was to her, at her ironing or mending, that I read my first Shakspere" (lines 42 and 43)
(2) " 'Don't love it so well, Clark, or it may be taken from you' " (lines 53 and 54)
(3) "I never knew how far it bore her, or past what happy islands" (lines 86 and 87)
(4) "Her lip quivered and she hastily put her handkerchief up to her mouth" (lines 81 and 82)   5 ____

6.   Lines 45 through 47 develop a central theme by
(1) recalling the husband's generosity in supporting the narrator's music lessons
(2) suggesting that the narrator resented his music lessons
(3) emphasizing the role of discipline in developing Aunt Georgiana's musical talent
(4) implying that Aunt Georgiana missed having music in her life   6 ____

7.   In line 49, when the narrator states that he "understood why," he is implying that his Aunt Georgiana
(1) knew little about current musical trends
(2) avoided talking about his musical skills
(3) realized what she has given up
(4) needed some recognition of her ability   7 ____

8.   Lines 59 through 66 contribute to a central idea by depicting Aunt Georgiana's
(1) concern for daily responsibilities   (3) fear of future separations
(2) desire for cultural experiences   (4) fixation on painful memories
                                                                                                       8 ____

9.   The author's choice of how to end the story (lines 92 through 98) places emphasis on Aunt Georgiana's
(1) bleak future   (3) domestic skills
(2) unusual lifestyle   (4) hostile attitude   9 ____

10. Which quotation best reflects the narrator's realization resulting from Aunt Georgiana's visit?
(1) "He requested me to meet her at the station and render her whatever services might be necessary" (lines 7 and 8)
(2) "At two o'clock the Symphony Orchestra was to give a Wagner program, and I intended to take my aunt" (lines 55 and 56)
(3) "there came to me an overwhelming sense of the waste and wear we are so powerless to combat" (lines 71 through 73)
(4) "sound poured on and on; I never knew what she found in the shining current of it" (lines 85 and 86)   10 ____

Mi Historia[1]

My red pickup choked on burnt oil
as I drove down Highway 99.[2]
In wind-tattered garbage bags
I had packed my whole life:
5   two pairs of jeans, a few T-shirts,
and a pair of work boots.
My truck needed work, and through
the blue smoke rising from under the hood,
I saw almond orchards, plums,
10 the raisins spread out on paper trays,
and acres of Mendota cotton my mother picked as a child.

My mother crawled through the furrows
and plucked cotton balls that filled
the burlap sack she dragged,
15 shoulder-slung, through dried-up bolls,
husks, weevils, dirt clods,
and dust that filled the air with thirst.
But when she grew tired,
she slept on her mother's burlap,
20 stuffed thick as a mattress,
and Grandma dragged her over the land
where time was told by the setting sun....

History cried out to me from the earth,
in the scream of starling flight,
25 and pounded at the hulls of seeds to be set free.
History licked the asphalt with rubber,
sighed in the windows of abandoned barns,
slumped in the wind-blasted palms,
groaned in the heat, and whispered its soft curses.
30 I wanted my own history—not the earth's,
nor the history of blood, nor of memory,
and not the job found for me at Galdini Sausage.
I sought my own—a new bruise to throb hard
as the asphalt that pounded the chassis of my truck.

—David Dominguez from *Work Done Right*, 2003
The University of Arizona Press

---

[1]Mi Historia — Spanish for "my history"
[2]Highway 99 — the highway that runs through California's fertile Central
Valley where generations of farmworkers have settled and been employed

. The poet's purpose in referencing "Highway 99" in line 2 is most likely to establish
(1) a connection with the narrator's cultural heritage
(2) a criticism of the valley's agricultural economy
(3) an understanding of the narrator's difficult childhood
(4) an emphasis on the region's diverse landscape   11 ___

12. The second stanza reveals that the narrator's overall point of view is influenced by
(1) his experience working on farms
(2) his nostalgia for farm life
(3) the labor of his relatives
(4) the expectations of his family   12 ___

13. The personification in lines 23 through 29 stresses history's desire to be
(1) repeated
(2) forgotten
(3) comforted
(4) heard   13 ___

14. The figurative language in lines 33 and 34 implies the narrator
(1) regrets leaving his past behind
(2) understands that his future will have challenges
(3) anticipates that his new life will be successful
(4) thinks he made a wrong decision   14 ___

Reading Comprehension Passage C

In 1973, a book claiming that plants were sentient[1] beings that feel emotions, prefer classical music to rock and roll, and can respond to the unspoken thoughts of humans hundreds of miles away landed on the New York *Times* best-seller list for nonfiction. "The Secret Life of Plants," by
5 Peter Tompkins and Christopher Bird, presented a beguiling mashup of legitimate plant science, quack experiments, and mystical nature worship that captured the public imagination at a time when New Age thinking was seeping into the mainstream. The most memorable passages described the experiments of a former C.I.A. polygraph expert named Cleve Backster,
10 who, in 1966, on a whim, hooked up a galvanometer to the leaf of a dracaena, a houseplant that he kept in his office. To his astonishment, Backster found that simply by imagining the dracaena being set on fire he could make it rouse the needle of the polygraph machine, registering a surge of electrical activity suggesting that the plant felt stress. "Could the
15 plant have been reading his mind?" the authors ask. "Backster felt like running into the street and shouting to the world, 'Plants can think!' " ...

In the ensuing years, several legitimate plant scientists tried to reproduce the "Backster effect" without success. Much of the science in "The Secret Life of Plants" has been discredited. But the book had
20 made its mark on the culture. Americans began talking to their plants and playing Mozart for them, and no doubt many still do. This might seem harmless enough; there will probably always be a strain of romanticism running through our thinking about plants. (Luther Burbank and George Washington Carver both reputedly talked to, and listened to, the plants
25 they did such brilliant work with.) But in the view of many plant scientists "The Secret Life of Plants" has done lasting damage to their field. According to Daniel Chamovitz, an Israeli biologist who is the author of the recent book "What a Plant Knows," Tompkins and Bird "stymied[2] important research on plant behavior as scientists became wary[3] of any
30 studies that hinted at parallels between animal senses and plant senses." Others contend that "The Secret Life of Plants" led to "self-censorship" among researchers seeking to explore the "possible homologies[4] between neurobiology[5] and phytobiology"[6]; that is, the possibility that plants are much more intelligent and much more like us than most
35 people think—capable of cognition,[7] communication, information processing, computation, learning and memory. ...

---

[1]sentient — conscious
[2]stymied — prevented
[3]wary — cautious
[4]homologies — similarities
[5]neurobiology — the study of the nervous system
[6]phytobiology — the study of plants
[7]cognition — understanding

Indeed, many of the most impressive capabilities of plants can be traced to their unique existential[8] predicament as beings rooted to the ground and therefore unable to pick up and move when they need some-
40 thing or when conditions turn unfavorable. The "sessile life style," as plant biologists term it, calls for an extensive and nuanced understanding of one's immediate environment, since the plant has to find everything it needs, and has to defend itself, while remaining fixed in place. A highly developed sensory apparatus is required to locate food and identify
45 threats. Plants have evolved between fifteen and twenty distinct senses, including analogues of our five: smell and taste (they sense and respond to chemicals in the air or on their bodies); sight (they react differently to various wavelengths of light as well as to shadow); touch (a vine or a root "knows" when it encounters a solid object); and, it has been discov-
50 ered, sound. In a recent experiment, Heidi Appel, a chemical ecologist at the University of Missouri, found that, when she played a recording of a caterpillar chomping a leaf for a plant that hadn't been touched, the sound primed the plant's genetic machinery to produce defense chemicals. Another experiment, done in Mancuso's[9] lab and not yet published, found
55 that plant roots would seek out a buried pipe through which water was flowing even if the exterior of the pipe was dry, which suggested that plants somehow "hear" the sound of flowing water. ...
Scientists have since found that the tips of the plant roots, in addition to sensing gravity, moisture, light, pressure, and hardness, can also
60 sense volume, nitrogen, phosphorus, salt, various toxins, microbes, and chemical signals from neighboring plants. Roots about to encounter an impenetrable obstacle or a toxic substance change course before they make contact with it. Roots can tell whether nearby roots are self or other and, if other, kin or stranger. Normally, plants compete for root space
65 with strangers, but, when researchers put four closely related Great Lakes sea-rocket plants (*Cakile edentula*) in the same pot, the plants restrained their usual competitive behaviors and shared resources.
Somehow, a plant gathers and integrates all this information about its environment, and then "decides"—some scientists deploy the quotation
70 marks, indicating metaphor at work; others drop them—in precisely what direction to deploy its roots or its leaves. Once the definition of "behavior" expands to include such things as a shift in the trajectory[10] of a root, a reallocation of resources, or the emission of a powerful chemical, plants begin to look like much more active agents, responding to environmental
75 cues in ways more subtle or adaptive than the word "instinct" would suggest. "Plants perceive competitors and grow away from them," Rick

[8]existential — relating to existence
[9]Mancuso — Stefano Mancuso, Italian plant physiologist
[10]trajectory — a path

Karban, a plant ecologist at U.C. Davis, explained, when I asked him for an example of plant decision-making. "They are more leery of actual vegetation than they are of inanimate objects, and they respond to
80 potential competitors before actually being shaded by them." These are sophisticated behaviors, but, like most plant behaviors, to an animal they're either invisible or really, really slow.

The sessile life style also helps account for plants' extraordinary gift for biochemistry, which far exceeds that of animals and, arguably, of
85 human chemists. (Many drugs, from aspirin to opiates, derive from compounds designed by plants.) Unable to run away, plants deploy a complex molecular vocabulary to signal distress, deter or poison enemies, and recruit animals to perform various services for them. A recent study in Science found that the caffeine produced by many plants may function
90 not only as a defense chemical, as had previously been thought, but in some cases as a psychoactive drug in their nectar. The caffeine encourages bees to remember a particular plant and return to it, making them more faithful and effective pollinators.

One of the most productive areas of plant research in recent years
95 has been plant signalling. Since the early nineteen-eighties, it has been known that when a plant's leaves are infected or chewed by insects they emit volatile chemicals that signal other leaves to mount a defense. Sometimes this warning signal contains information about the identity of the insect, gleaned from the taste of its saliva. Depending on the plant
100 and the attacker, the defense might involve altering the leaf's flavor or texture, or producing toxins or other compounds that render the plant's flesh less digestible to herbivores. When antelopes browse acacia trees, the leaves produce tannins that make them unappetizing and difficult to digest. When food is scarce and acacias are overbrowsed, it has been
105 reported, the trees produce sufficient amounts of toxin to kill the animals. ...

All species face the same existential challenges—obtaining food, defending themselves, reproducing—but under wildly varying circumstances, and so they have evolved wildly different tools in order to survive. Brains come in handy for creatures that move around a lot;
110 but they're a disadvantage for ones that are rooted in place. Impressive as it is to us, self-consciousness is just another tool for living, good for some jobs, unhelpful for others. That humans would rate this particular adaptation so highly is not surprising, since it has been the shining destination of our long evolutionary journey, along with the
115 epiphenomenon of self-consciousness that we call "free will." ...

—Michael Pollan excerpted from "The Intelligent Plant"
The New Yorker, December 23 & 30, 2013

15. The first paragraph conveys a sense of
(1) caution   (2) accusation   (3) excitement   (4) relief   15 ___

16. The details in the first paragraph serve mainly to establish the
(1) relationship between plant science and musical trends
(2) difference between houseplants and wild plants
(3) importance of forensic science for theories of plant behavior
(4) impact of early studies of plant behavior on current research   16 ___

17. The author uses the word "But" in line 19 to
(1) express the controversial nature of "The Secret Life of Plants"
(2) compare "The Secret Life of Plants" with "What a Plant Knows"
(3) express the similarities between certain types of plants
(4) compare the learning ability of particular types of plants   17 ___

18. A primary purpose of the details in lines 45 through 50 is to
indicate a connection
(1) among diverse plant species
(2) among several independent studies
(3) between humans and plants
(4) between predators and prey   18 ___

19. The use of quotation marks in lines 69 and 71 acknowledges
the presence of
(1) deception   (2) debate   (3) confusion   (4) resentment   19 ___

20. Lines 71 through 76 support a central idea suggesting that plants
(1) resist cooperation   (3) produce sound
(2) avoid modification   (4) possess intent   20 ___

21. The evidence provided in lines 88 through 93 demonstrates
that plants may
(1) develop symbiotic relationships (3) waste essential resources
(2) attack weaker organisms   (4) produce genetic mutations   21 ___

22. The term "plant signalling" (line 95) refers to the way plants
(1) reproduce with similar species
(2) protect themselves from predators
(3) react to human contact
(4) adapt themselves to climate   22 ___

23. The final paragraph contributes to a central idea by suggesting that
(1) humans have acquired superior characteristics
(2) species develop according to their own needs
(3) plants would benefit from having self-awareness
(4) scientists have dismissed important findings   23 ___

24. The text's credibility relies on the author's use of
(1) order of importance   (3) observable evidence
(2) extended comparison   (4) personal anecdotes   24 ___

Part 2
Argument

Directions: Closely read each of the *four* texts provided on the following pages and write a source-based argument on the topic below. You may use the margins to take notes as you read and scrap paper to plan your response. Write your argument on a separate sheet of paper provided by the teacher.

Topic: Should school recess be structured play?

Your Task: Carefully read each of the *four* texts provided. Then, using evidence from at least *three* of the texts, write a well-developed argument regarding whether or not school recess should be structured play. Clearly establish your claim, distinguish your claim from alternate or opposing claims, and use specific, relevant, and sufficient evidence from at least *three* of the texts to develop your argument. Do not simply summarize each text.

Guidelines:
  Be sure to:
   • Establish your claim regarding whether or not school recess should be structured play
   • Distinguish your claim from alternate or opposing claims
   • Use specific, relevant, and sufficient evidence from at least *three* of the texts to develop your argument
   • Identify each source that you reference by text number and line number(s) or graphic (for example: Text 1, line 4 or Text 2, graphic)
   • Organize your ideas in a cohesive and coherent manner
   • Maintain a formal style of writing
   • Follow the conventions of standard written English

Texts:
   Text 1 – The Crucial Role of Recess in School
   Text 2 – Why Children Need More Unstructured Play
   Text 3 – Study Weighs Benefits of Organizing Recess
   Text 4 – Forget Goofing Around: Recess Has a New Boss

Text 1
The Crucial Role of Recess in School

...Structured recess is a recess based on structured play, during which games and physical activities are taught and led by a trained adult (teachers, school staff, or volunteers). Proponents[1] for structured recess note that children often need help in developing games and require
5   suggestions and encouragement to participate in physical activities. Recently, policy makers and funding organizations have called for more opportunities for daily activity as a means to address childhood obesity. These statements have strengthened the argument to maintain or reinstate recess as an integral component of the school day. Although this new
10   dimension to the recess debate has increased attention on its role, it also has created tension. Some have promoted recess time as a solution for increasing children's physical activity and combating obesity. If recess assumes such a role, then, like physical education, it will need to be planned and directed to ensure that all children are participating in
15   moderately vigorous physical activity. Pediatric health care providers, parents, and school officials should be cognizant,[2] however, that in designing a structured recess, they will sacrifice the notion of recess as an unstructured but supervised break that belongs to the child; that is, a time for the child to make a personal choice between sedentary, physical,
20   creative, or social options. However, there are many cited benefits of structured recess to consider, including:

- Older elementary children may benefit from game instruction and encouragement for total class inclusion.
- Children can be coached to develop interpersonal skills for
25   appropriate conflict resolution.
- More children can actively participate in regular activity, irrespective of skill level.
- Anecdotally,[3] teachers have reported improved behavior and attention in the classroom after vigorous structured recess.

30   To be effective, structured recess requires that school personnel (or volunteers) receive adequate training so that they are able to address and encourage the diverse needs of all students. One aspect of supervision should be to facilitate social relationships among children by encouraging inclusiveness in games. A problem arises when the structured activities of
35   recess are promoted as a replacement for the child's physical education requirement. The replacement of physical education by recess threatens students' instruction in and acquisition of new motor skills, exploration of sports and rules, and a concept of lifelong physical fitness.

---

[1]proponents — those who support
[2]cognizant — aware
[3]anecdotally — based on casual observation

There are ways to encourage a physically active recess without
40   necessarily adding structured, planned, adult-led games, such as offering
attractive, safe playground equipment to stimulate free play; establishing
games/boundaries painted on the playground; or instructing children
in games, such as four square or hop-scotch. These types of activities
can range from fully structured (with the adult directing and requiring
45   participation) to partly unstructured (with adults providing supervision
and initial instruction) to fully unstructured (supervision and social
guidance). In structured, partly structured, or unstructured environments,
activity levels vary widely on the basis of school policy, equipment
provided, encouragement, age group, gender, and race. Consequently, the
50   potential benefits of mandatory participation of all children in a purely
structured recess must be weighed against the potential social and
emotional trade-off of limiting acquisition of important developmental
skills. Whichever style is chosen, recess should be viewed as a supplement
to motor skill acquisition in physical education class. ...

                                   —Council on School Health
excerpted from "The Crucial Role of Recess in School," December 31, 2012
                                 http://pediatrics.aapublications.org/

Text 2
Why Children Need More Unstructured Play

The nature of an average child's free time has changed. For the past 25
years kids have been spending decreasing amounts of time outdoors. The
time that our kids do spend outdoors is frequently a part of an organized
sports activity. Other activities taking up our children's time include
5   indoor lessons and organized events such as music, art and dance lessons.
Another big indoor activity, taking up to 7.5 hours a day of our children's
time according to a Kaiser Family Foundation study, is electronic
entertainment. Of course some of these activities bring joy and
fulfillment to our kids, but, in return, time for unstructured play has
10   decreased.

Unstructured play is that set of activities that children create on their
own without adult guidance. Children naturally, when left to their own
devices, will take initiative and create activities and stories in the world
around them. Sometimes, especially with children past the toddler stage,
15   the most creative play takes place outside of direct adult supervision.
Unstructured free play can happen in many different environments,
however, the outdoors may provide more opportunities for free play due
to the many movable parts, such as sticks, dirt, leaves and rocks which
lend themselves to exploration and creation.

20   Some parents find it challenging to provide unstructured play time for their kids. Letting our kids play without constant supervision, especially outside, can be even more difficult. It feels hard to balance reasonable concern, over-vigilance, and the desire to let our kids experience freedom and learn from their own mistakes and experiences. ...

25   Why might we need to loosen up and get over some of our fears in order to get our kids outdoor unstructured play time? In the January 2005 *Archives of Pediatric and Adolescent Medicine*, Burdette and Whitaker wrote on the importance of free play. They argue that free play promotes intellectual and cognitive growth, emotional intelligence, and benefits

30   social interactions. They describe how play involves problem solving which is one of the highest executive functions. ["]Children plan, organize, sequence, and make decisions,["] they explain. In addition, play requires attention to the game and, especially in the case of very young children, frequent physical activity. Unstructured play frequently

35   comes from or results in exposure to the outdoors. Surveys of parents and teachers report that children's focus and attention are improved after outdoor physical activity and free play and some small studies suggest that time spent outdoors improves focus in children with ADHD [Attention Deficit Hyperactivity Disorder].

40   Socialization and emotional intelligence benefit through shared interactions and physical movement that take place during play. Children must work together to decide which game to play, what agreeable rules are, and how to manage scenarios that invariably involve their differing perspectives. This "work" builds the social qualities that we all wish for

45   our children: empathy, self-awareness, self-regulation, and flexibility. Emotional development is promoted along with physical health when people spend time moving. In adults and older children physical activity has been well documented to decrease stress, anxiety, and depression, and to improve overall mood. Though the research is sparse in younger

50   children, it seems likely that our youngest children benefit as well. Free play in toddlers and young children most frequently involves spurts of gross motor activity over a period of time with multiple episodes of rest in between. Most children are smiling and laughing when they engage in play, and it is reasonable to assume that their mood is improved

55   during and after play. ...

       —Avril Swan, MD excerpted and adapted from "Why Children Need More Unstructured Play" www.kevinmd.com, July 21, 2011

Text 3
Study Weighs Benefits of Organizing Recess

While an overwhelming number of elementary school principals believe in the power of recess to improve academic achievement and make students more focused in class, most discipline-related problems happen at school when kids cut loose at recess and lunch, according to
5   surveys.

One of the solutions, according to a study released this week [2012] by the Robert Wood Johnson Foundation: more, and well-trained, staff on the playground.

The study examines an approach to creating more-structured recess
10   time that is provided by Playworks, based in Oakland, Calif. It finds that the nonprofit organization's program can smooth the transition between recess and class time—giving teachers more time to spend on instruction—and can cut back on bullying in the schoolyard. Teachers in participating schools also reported that their students felt safer and
15   more included at recess, compared with those at schools without the program. ...

The most significant finding shows students who participate in a Playworks-structured recess transition from that to schoolwork more quickly than students in traditional recess, said Susanne James-Burdumy,
20   an associate director of research at Mathematica Policy Research.

"I think it is an exciting set of findings," Ms. James-Burdumy said. "This is one area where Playworks is aiming to have an impact: specifically trying to improve students' ability to focus on class activities."

The study found that, on average, teachers at participating schools
25   needed about 2.5 fewer minutes of transition time between recess and learning time—a difference that researchers termed statistically significant. Over the course of a school year, that can add up to about a day of class time.

Scaling Up

The Robert Wood Johnson Foundation, also based in Princeton, has
30   been funding Playworks since 2005. It helped the program expand from a few schools in Oakland to more than 300 schools in 23 cities, said Nancy Barrand, the foundation's senior adviser for program development. The goal is to expand into 27 cities and 750 schools.

"We're using a process of scaling where we've identified a successful,
35   evidence-based model," Ms. Barrand said. Playworks "is a pretty common-sense approach. It's really about the school environment and how you create a healthy school environment for the children," she continued. "If children are healthy and happy, they learn better."

Playworks founder and chief executive officer, Jill Vialet, said the
40   idea came from a frustrated principal 15 years ago. The principal had been dealing with the same three students daily because of scuffles and mischief at recess that spilled over into their classes.

Ms. Vialet wondered whether creating a little structure at recess could quell some of those ongoing woes. She recalled her own days as a child

45   when a municipal parks and recreation worker named Clarence made sure she—one of the few girls there—was included in the games at a District of Columbia park.

"I wanted to make sure every kid had a Clarence," she said. ...

The coaches map the area where students spend recess, setting

50   boundaries for different activities, such as kickball. They help children pick teams using random measures, such as students' birth months, to circumvent emotionally scarring episodes of being chosen based on skill or popularity. If conflicts arise, coaches teach simple ways to settle disputes and preempt some quibbles by teaching games including rock-

55   paper-scissors.

Forty percent of the surveyed teachers said students used the rock-paper-scissors game to resolve conflicts or make decisions when they were back in class.

Coaches get involved in the activities, which "makes it possible

60   for kids who don't see themselves as super-sporty to get into the games themselves," Ms. Vialet said. "There's just enough structure for the kids to be successful."

Solving Own Problems

While adults need to be present and ready to intervene at recess if necessary, said Edward Miller, one of the founding partners of the

65   New York City-based Alliance for Childhood, and Playworks provides that service, children should also have the opportunity for individual and small-group play. ...

The Mathematica study found Playworks has a mixed effect on behaviors related to bullying: Teachers at schools with the program

70   found that there was significantly less bullying and exclusionary behavior during recess than teachers at schools without it, but not a reduction in more general aggressive behavior. Playworks has no formal curriculum that addresses the problem, Ms. Vialet noted.

"Our coaches are functioning like the older kids in the play yard used

75   to: teaching kids rules to games, intervening if there is conflict, norming[1] behaviors around inclusion," she said.

However, researchers also found that teachers' and students' perception of aggression and bullying on the playground differed. While teachers observed that there was less name-calling, shoving of

80   classmates, and excluding of some students from games because of Playworks, students didn't, Mathematica's Ms. James-Burdumy said. ...

—Nirvi Shah

excerpted and adapted from "Study Weighs Benefits of Organizing Recess"
www.edweek.org, April 17, 2012

---

[1]norming — setting a standard

Text 4
Forget Goofing Around: Recess Has a New Boss

Newark — At Broadway Elementary School here, there is no more sitting around after lunch. No more goofing off with friends. No more doing nothing.

Instead there is Brandi Parker, a $14-an-hour recess coach with a
5   whistle around her neck, corralling children behind bright orange cones to play organized games. There she was the other day, breaking up a renegade game of hopscotch and overruling stragglers' lame excuses.

They were bored. They had tired feet. They were no good at running.

"I don't like to play," protested Esmeilyn Almendarez, 11.
10   "Why do I have to go through this every day with you?" replied Ms. Parker, waving her back in line. "There's no choice."

Broadway Elementary brought in Ms. Parker in January out of exasperation with students who, left to their own devices, used to run into one another, squabble over balls and jump-ropes or monopolize
15   the blacktop while exiling their classmates to the sidelines. Since she started, disciplinary referrals at recess have dropped by three-quarters, to an average of three a week. And injuries are no longer a daily occurrence.

"Before, I was seeing nosebleeds, busted lips, and students being a
20   danger to themselves and others," said Alejandro Echevarria, the principal. "Now, Coach Brandi does miracles with 20 cones and three handballs."

The school is one of a growing number across the country that are reining in recess to curb bullying and behavior problems, foster social
25   skills and address concerns over obesity. They also hope to show children that there is good old-fashioned fun to be had without iPods and video games. ...

Although many school officials and parents like the organized activity, its critics say it takes away the only time that children have to unwind. ...
30   Dr. Romina M. Barros, an assistant clinical professor at Albert Einstein College of Medicine in the Bronx who was an author of a widely cited study on the benefits of recess, published last year [2009] in the journal Pediatrics, says that children still benefit most from recess when they are let alone to daydream, solve problems, use their imagination
35   to invent their own games and "be free to do what they choose to do."

Structured recess, Dr. Barros said, simply transplants the rules of the classroom to the playground.

"You still have to pay attention," she said. "You still have to follow rules. You don't have that time for your brain to relax." ...
40   Ms. Parker, 28, the coach at Broadway Elementary, had worked as a counselor for troubled teenagers in a group home in Burlington, N.C. Besides her work at recess, she visits each class once a week to play games that teach lessons about cooperation, sportsmanship and respect.

"These are the things that matter in life: who you are as a human being
45   at the core," she said. ...

There are three 15-minute recesses, with more than 100 children at a
time packed into a fenced-in basketball court equipped with nothing
more than a pair of netless hoops.

On a chilly morning, Ms. Parker shoveled snow off the blacktop so
50   that the students could go outside after being cooped up in the cafeteria
during recess in the previous week. She drew squares in blue and green
chalk for a game called switch, a fast-paced version of musical chairs
— without the chairs. (She goes through a box of chalk a week.)

Ms. Parker, who greets students with hugs and a cheerful "hello-hello,"
55   keeps the rules simple so that they can focus on playing rather than on
following directions. "We're trying to get them to exert energy, to get it
all out," she said. "They can be as loud as they want. I never tell them
to be quiet unless I'm telling them something." ...

—Winnie Hu
excerpted and adapted from "Forget Goofing Around: Recess Has a New
Boss" www.nytimes.com, March 14, 2010

Part 3
Text-Analysis Response

Your Task: Closely read the text provided on the following pages and write
a well-developed, text-based response of two to three paragraphs. In your
response, identify a central idea in the text and analyze how the author's use
of *one* writing strategy (literary element or literary technique or rhetorical
device) develops this central idea. Use strong and thorough evidence from the
text to support your analysis. Do *not* simply summarize the text. You may
use the margins to take notes as you read and scrap paper to plan your
response. Write your response on a separate sheet of paper.

Guidelines:
  Be sure to:
  • Identify a central idea in the text
  • Analyze how the author's use of *one* writing strategy (literary element
    or literary technique or rhetorical device) develops this central idea.
    Examples include: characterization, conflict, denotation/connotation,
    metaphor, simile, irony, language use, point-of-view, setting, structure,
    symbolism, theme, tone, etc.
  • Use strong and thorough evidence from the text to support your analysis
  • Organize your ideas in a cohesive and coherent manner
  • Maintain a formal style of writing
  • Follow the conventions of standard written English

Text

The following excerpt from the memoir of a South Pole explorer includes quotations from his diary.

...Then came a fateful day — Wednesday, October 27. The position was lat. [latitude] 69° 5' S., long. [longitude] 51° 30' W. The temperature was −8.5° Fahr. [Fahrenheit], a gentle southerly breeze was blowing and the sun shone in a clear sky. "After long months of ceaseless anxiety and

5   strain, after times when hope beat high and times when the outlook was black indeed, the end of the *Endurance* has come. But though we have been compelled to abandon the ship, which is crushed beyond all hope of ever being righted, we are alive and well, and we have stores and equipment for the task that lies before us. The task is to reach land with all the members

10   of the Expedition. It is hard to write what I feel. To a sailor his ship is more than a floating home, and in the *Endurance* I had centred ambitions, hopes, and desires. Now, straining and groaning, her timbers cracking and her wounds gaping, she is slowly giving up her sentient[1] life at the very outset of her career. She is crushed and abandoned after drifting more

15   than 570 miles in a north-westerly direction during the 281 days since she became locked in the ice. The distance from the point where she became beset[2] to the place where she now rests mortally hurt in the grip of the floes[3] is 573 miles, but the total drift through all observed positions has been 1186 miles, and probably we actually covered more than 1500 miles.

20   We are now 346 miles from Paulet Island, the nearest point where there is any possibility of finding food and shelter. A small hut built there by the Swedish expedition in 1902 is filled with stores left by the Argentine relief ship. I know all about those stores, for I purchased them in London on behalf of the Argentine Government when they asked me to equip the relief

25   expedition. The distance to the nearest barrier west of us is about 180 miles, but a party going there would still be about 360 miles from Paulet Island and there would be no means of sustaining life on the barrier. We could not take from here food enough for the whole journey; the weight would be too great.

30   "This morning, our last on the ship, the weather was clear, with a gentle south-southeasterly to south-south-westerly breeze. From the crow's-nest there was no sign of land of any sort. The pressure was increasing steadily, and the passing hours brought no relief or respite[4] for the ship. The attack of the ice reached its climax at 4 p.m. The ship was hove[5] stern up by the

35   pressure, and the driving floe, moving laterally across the stern, split the rudder and tore out the rudder-post and stern-post. Then, while we watched, the ice loosened and the *Endurance* sank a little. The decks were breaking

---

[1]sentient — conscious
[2]beset — hemmed in
[3]floes — ice sheets
[4]respite — rest
[5]hove — heaved

upwards and the water was pouring in below. Again the pressure began, and
at 5 p.m. I ordered all hands on to the ice. The twisting, grinding floes were
40   working their will at last on the ship. It was a sickening sensation to feel
the decks breaking up under one's feet, the great beams bending and then
snapping with a noise like heavy gunfire. The water was overmastering the
pumps, and so to avoid an explosion when it reached the boilers I had to
give orders for the fires to be drawn[6] and the steam let down. The plans for
45   abandoning the ship in case of emergency had been made well in advance,
and men and dogs descended to the floe and made their way to the
comparative safety of an unbroken portion of the floe without a hitch.
Just before leaving, I looked down the engine-room skylight as I stood on
the quivering deck, and saw the engines dropping sideways as the stays
50   and bed-plates gave way. I cannot describe the impression of relentless
destruction that was forced upon me as I looked down and around. The
floes, with the force of millions of tons of moving ice behind them, were
simply annihilating the ship." …
       "To-night the temperature has dropped to –16° Fahr., and most of the men
55   are cold and uncomfortable. After the tents had been pitched I mustered
all hands and explained the position to them briefly and, I hope, clearly. I
have told them the distance to the barrier and the distance to Paulet Island,
and have stated that I propose to try to march with equipment across the
ice in the direction of Paulet Island. I thanked the men for the steadiness
60   and good *morale* they have shown in these trying circumstances, and told
them I had no doubt that, provided they continued to work their utmost and
to trust me, we will all reach safety in the end. Then we had supper, which
the cook had prepared at the big blubber stove, and after a watch[7] had been
set all hands except the watch turned in." For myself, I could not sleep.
65   The destruction and abandonment of the ship was no sudden shock. The
disaster had been looming ahead for many months, and I had studied my
plans for all contingencies[8] a hundred times. But the thoughts that came
to me as I walked up and down in the darkness were not particularly cheerful.
The task now was to secure the safety of the party, and to that I must bend
70   my energies and mental power and apply every bit of knowledge that
experience of the Antarctic had given me. The task was likely to be long and
strenuous, and an ordered mind and a clear programme were essential if we
were to come through without loss of life. A man must shape himself to
a new mark directly the old one goes to ground. …

—Sir Ernest Shackleton
excepted and adapted from *South*, 1920
The MacMillan Company

---

[6]drawn — closed
[7]watch — crewman who stays awake on guard all night
[8]contingencies — possibilities

August 2017
Part 1
Multiple-Choice Questions

Directions (1–24): Closely read each of the three passages below. After each passage, there are several multiple choice questions. Select the best suggested answer to each question and record your answer in the space provided. You may use the margins to take notes as you read.

Reading Comprehension Passage A

In this passage, Dora-Rouge, a Native American Indian elder, is traveling back to her homeland by canoe with a small group of women.

...As we traveled, we entered time and began to trouble it, to pester it apart or into some kind of change. On the short nights we sat by firelight and looked at the moon's long face on water. Dora-Rouge would lie on the beaver blankets and tell us what place we would pass on the next
5 day. She'd look at the stars in the shortening night and say, "the Meeting Place," or "God Island." True to her word, the next day we reached those places. ...

Now, looking back, I understand how easily we lost track of things. The time we'd been teasing apart, unraveled. And now it began to unravel
10 us as we entered a kind of timelessness. Wednesday was the last day we called by name, and truly, we no longer needed time. We were lost from it, and lost in this way, I came alive. It was as if I'd slept for years, and was now awake. The others felt it, too. Cell by cell, all of us were taken in by water and by land, swallowed a little at a time. What we'd thought
15 of as our lives and being on earth was gone, and now the world was made up of pathways of its own invention. We were only one of the many dreams of earth. And I knew we were just a small dream.

But there was a place inside the human that spoke with land, that entered dreaming, in the way that people in the north found direction in
20 their dreams. They dreamed charts of land and currents of water. They dreamed where food animals lived. These dreams they called hunger maps and when they followed those maps, they found their prey. It was the language animals and humans had in common. People found their cures in the same way. ...
25 For my own part in this dreaming, as soon as I left time, when Thursday and Friday slipped away, plants began to cross my restless sleep in abundance. A tendril reached through darkness, a first sharp leaf came up from the rich ground of my sleeping, opened upward from the place in my body that knew absolute truth. It wasn't a seed that had been
30 planted there, not a cultivated growing, but a wild one, one that had been there all along, waiting. I saw vines creeping forward. Inside the thin lid of an eye, petals opened, and there was pollen at the center of each flower. Field, forest, swamp. I knew how they breathed at night, and that they were linked to us in that breath. It was the oldest bond of survival.

35 I was devoted to woods the wind walked through, to mosses and lichens. Somewhere in my past, I had lost the knowing of this opening light of life, the taking up of minerals from dark ground, the magnitude of thickets and brush. Now I found it once again. Sleep changed me. I remembered things I'd forgotten, how a hundred years ago, leaves reached
40 toward sunlight, plants bent into currents of water. Something persistent nudged me and it had morning rain on its leaves.

Maybe the roots of dreaming are in the soil of dailiness, or in the heart, or in another place without words, but when they come together and grow, they are like the seeds of hydrogen and the seeds of oxygen that together
45 create ocean, lake, and ice. In this way, the plants and I joined each other. They entangled me in their stems and vines and it was a beautiful entanglement. ...

Some mornings as we packed our things, set out across water, the world was the color of copper, a flood of sun arrived from the east, and
50 a thick mist rose up from black earth. Other mornings, heating water over the fire, we'd see the world covered with fog, and the birdsongs sounded forlorn and far away. There were days when we traveled as many as thirty miles. Others we traveled no more than ten. There were times when I resented the work, and days I worked so hard even Agnes' liniment
55 and aspirin would not relax my aching shoulders and I would crave ice, even a single chip of it, cold and shining. On other days I felt a deep contentment as I poled[1] inside shallow currents or glided across a new wide lake.

We were in the hands of nature. In these places things turned about
60 and were other than what they seemed. In silence, I pulled through the water and saw how a river appeared through rolling fog and emptied into the lake. One day, a full-tailed fox moved inside the shadows of trees, then stepped into a cloud. New senses came to me. I was equal to the other animals, hearing as they heard, moving as they moved, seeing
65 as they saw.

One night we stayed on an island close to the decaying, moss-covered pieces of a boat. Its remains looked like the ribs of a large animal. In the morning, sun was a dim light reaching down through the branches of trees. Pollen floated across the dark water and gathered, yellow and
70 life-giving, along the place where water met land. ...

One evening it seemed cooler. The air had a different feel, rarefied, clean, and thin. Wolves in the distance were singing and their voices made a sound that seemed to lie upon the land, like a cloud covering the world from one edge of the horizon to the other. We sat around the fire and
75 listened, the light on our faces, our eyes soft. Agnes warmed her hands over the flames.

There was a shorter time of darkness every night, but how beautiful the brief nights, with the stars and the wolves. ...

---

[1]poled — propelled a boat with a pole

Sometimes I felt there were eyes around us, peering through trees
80 and fog. Maybe it was the eyes of land and creatures regarding us, taking
our measure. And listening to the night, I knew there was another horizon,
beyond the one we could see. And all of it was storied land, land where
deities[2] walked, where people traveled, desiring to be one with infinite
space.
85   We were full and powerful, wearing the face of the world, floating in
silence. Dora-Rouge said, "Yes, I believe we've always been lost," as we
traveled through thick-grown rushes, marsh, and water so shallow our
paddles touched bottom.
    The four of us became like one animal. We heard inside each other in
90 a tribal way. I understood this at once and was easy with it. With my
grandmothers, there was no such thing as loneliness. Before, my life had
been without all its ears, eyes, without all its knowings. Now we, the four
of us, all had the same eyes, and when Dora-Rouge pointed a bony finger
and said, "This way," we instinctively followed that crooked finger.
95   I never felt lost. I felt newly found, opening, like the tiny eggs we found
in a pond one day, fertile and transparent. I bent over them. The life was
already moving inside them, like an eye or heartbeat. One day we passed
alongside cliff walls that bore red, ancient drawings of moose and bear.
These were said to have been painted not by humans, but by spirits. ...

—Linda Hogan
excerpted from *"Solar Storms,"* 1995
Scribner

———————————
[2]deities — gods

1.   In lines 3 through 7, the narrator portrays Dora-Rouge as
(1) compassionate   (3) knowledgeable
(2) detached   (4) misguided   1 ____

2.   In lines 16 and 17, the narrator compares people's lives to dreams in
order to illustrate the idea of
(1) resourcefulness   (3) vulnerability
(2) individuality   (4) insignificance   2 ____

3.   Which phrase from the text best illustrates the meaning of "tendril"
as used in line 27?
(1) "I saw vines creeping forward" (line 31)
(2) "there was pollen at the center" (line 32)
(3) "Field, forest, swamp" (line 33)
(4) "woods the wind walked through" (line 35)   3 ____

4.   The imagery in lines 31 through 35 can best be described as
(1) amusing   (2) threatening   (3) confusing   (4) enlightening 4 ____

5. The description in lines 59 through 65 creates a sense of
(1) transformation (2) isolation (3) division (4) vindication   5 _____

6. The phrase, "We were full and powerful, wearing the face of
the world," (line 85) suggests that the group
(1) believed they were something they were not
(2) developed a kinship with the environment
(3) became outwardly proud and aggressive
(4) adopted a casual attitude toward nature   6 _____

7. The language use in lines 95 through 99 serves to
(1) link the past with the future
(2) continue an ongoing struggle
(3) present a cultural dilemma
(4) clarify the need for cooperation   7 _____

8. The passage is primarily developed through the use of
(1) rhetorical questions   (3) parallel structure
(2) comparison and contrast   (4) personal narrative   8 _____

9. The passage as a whole supports the theme that with
(1) approval of society comes cultural freedom
(2) clarity of mind comes connection of spirit
(3) support of others comes environmental change
(4) passage of time comes acceptance of nature   9 _____

10. Which quotation best supports a central idea of the passage?
(1) "Maybe the roots of dreaming are in the soil of dailiness" (line 42)
(2) "On other days I felt a deep contentment as I poled inside shallow
currents or glided across a new wide lake" (lines 56 through 58)
(3) "The air had a different feel, rarefied, clean, and thin" (lines 71 and 72)
(4) "And listening to the night, I knew there was another horizon,
beyond the one we could see" (lines 81 and 82)   10 _____

Reading Comprehension Passage B
I Am Vertical

But I would rather be horizontal.
I am not a tree with my root in the soil
Sucking up minerals and motherly love
So that each March I may gleam into leaf,
5   Nor am I the beauty of a garden bed
Attracting my share of Ahs and spectacularly painted,
Unknowing I must soon unpetal.
Compared with me, a tree is immortal
And a flower-head not tall, but more startling,
10 And I want the one's longevity and the other's daring.

Tonight, in the infinitesimal[1] light of the stars,
The trees and flowers have been strewing their cool odors.
I walk among them, but none of them are noticing.
Sometimes I think that when I am sleeping
15 I must most perfectly resemble them—
Thoughts gone dim.
It is more natural to me, lying down.
Then the sky and I are in open conversation,
And I shall be useful when I lie down finally:
20 Then the trees may touch me for once, and the flowers
have time for me.

—Sylvia Plath
from *Uncollected Poems*, 1965
Turret Books

----

[1]infinitesimal — very small

11. The word "unpetal" in line 7 suggests
(1) inspiration   (2) invisibility   (3) isolation   (4) impermanence   11 ___

12. Lines 11 through 13 reveal the narrator's awareness of
(1) the limited time people exist on earth
(2) the unexpected changes that affect one's life
(3) her anxiety over the shifting of seasons
(4) her insignificance in the eyes of nature   12 ___

13. In lines 14 through 16, the narrator suggests that
(1) consciousness is a barrier to connecting with nature
(2) nature's ability to impress surpasses human's imagination
(3) the future depends on natural forces beyond human control
(4) nature's cruelty causes one to feel helpless   13 ___

14. Throughout the poem, the tone can best be described as
(1) envious   (2) skeptical   (3) hostile   (4) indignant   14 ___

Reading Comprehension Passage C

Jian Lin was 14 years old in 1973, when the Chinese government under Mao Zedong recruited him for a student science team called "the earthquake watchers." After a series of earthquakes that had killed thousandsin northern China, the country's seismologists[1] thought that
5 if they augmented[2] their own research by having observers keep an eye out for anomalies like snakes bolting early from their winter dens and erratic[3] well-water levels, they might be able to do what no scientific body had managed before: issue an earthquake warning that would save thousands of lives.
10   In the winter of 1974, the earthquake watchers were picking up some suspicious signals near the city of Haicheng. Panicked chickens were squalling and trying to escape their pens; water levels were falling in wells. Seismologists had also begun noticing a telltale pattern of small quakes. "They were like popcorn kernels," Lin tells me, "popping up all over
15 the general area." Then, suddenly, the popping stopped, just as it had before a catastrophic earthquake in 1966 that killed more than 8,000. "Like 'the calm before the storm,'" Lin says. "We have that exact same phrase in Chinese." On the morning of February 4, 1975, the seismology bureau issued a warning: Haicheng should expect a big earthquake,
20 and people should move outdoors.
     At 7:36 p.m., a magnitude 7.0 quake struck. The city was nearly leveled, but only about 2,000 people were killed. Without the warning, easily 150,000 would have died. "And so you finally had an earthquake forecast that did indeed save lives," Lin recalls. "People were excited. Or, you
25 could say, uplifted. *Uplifted* is a great word for it." But uplift turned to heartbreak the very next year, when a 7.5 quake shattered the city of Tangshan without so much as a magnitude 4 to introduce it. When the quake hit the city of 1.6 million at 3:42 a.m., it killed nearly 250,000 people, most of whom were asleep. "If there was any moment in my life
30 when I was scared of earthquakes, that was it," Lin says. "You think, what if it happened to you? And it could. I decided that if I could do anything —*anything*—to save lives lost to earthquakes, it would be worth the effort."
     Lin is now a senior scientist of geophysics at Woods Hole Oceanographic Institution, in Massachusetts, where he spends his time
35 studying not the scurrying of small animals and fluctuating electrical current between trees (another fabled warning sign), but seismometer readings, GPS coordinates, and global earthquake-notification reports. He and his longtime collaborator, Ross Stein of the U.S. Geological Survey, are champions of a theory that could enable scientists to forecast earth-
40 quakes with more precision and speed.

---

[1]seismologists — people who study earthquakes
[2]augmented — added to
[3]erratic — unpredictable
[4]geophysicists — people who study the physics of the earth and its environment, including seismology

Some established geophysicists[4] insist that all earthquakes are random, yet everyone agrees that aftershocks are not. Instead, they follow certain empirical laws. Stein, Lin, and their collaborators hypothesized that many earthquakes classified as main shocks are actually aftershocks, and they
45 went looking for the forces that cause faults to fail.

Their work was in some ways heretical[5]: For a long time, earthquakes were thought to release only the stress immediately around them; an earthquake that happened in one place would decrease the possibility of another happening nearby. But that didn't explain earthquake sequences
50 like the one that rumbled through the desert and mountains east of Los Angeles in 1992. The series began on April 23 with a 6.2 near the town of Joshua Tree; two months later, on June 28, a 7.3 struck less than 15 miles away in the desert town of Landers. Three and a half hours after that, a 6.5 hit the town of Big Bear, in the mountains overlooking the
55 Mojave. The Big Bear quake was timed like an aftershock, except it was too far off the Landers earthquake's fault rupture. When Lin, Stein, and Geoffrey King of the Paris Geophysical Institute got together to analyze it, they decided to ignore the distance rule and treat it just as a different kind of aftershock. Their ensuing report, "Static Stress Changes and
60 the Triggering of Earthquakes," became one of the decade's most-cited earthquake research papers.

Rocks can be subject to two kinds of stresses: the "clamping" stress that pushes them together, and the "shear" stress they undergo as they slide past each other. Together, these stresses are known as Coulomb stress,
65 named for Charles-Augustin de Coulomb, an 18th century French physicist. Coulomb calculations had been used for years in engineering, to find the failure points of various building materials, but they'd never been applied properly to faults. It turned out, though, that faults in the ground behave much like rocks in the laboratory: they come unglued when
70 shear stress exceeds the friction and pressure (the clamping stress) holding them together. When Stein, Lin, and King applied the Coulomb model to the California sequence, they found that most of the earthquakes had occurred in areas where the shifting of the ground had caused increased stress.

75   In 1997, Stein and two other geologists using the model found that there was a 12 percent chance that a magnitude 7 or greater would hit near Izmit, Turkey, within 30 years; two years later, on August 17, 1999, a magnitude 7.4 destroyed the city, which wasn't designed to withstand such a tremor. A Turkish geologist named Aykut Barka quickly wrote up
80 a paper warning that Coulomb stress from the Izmit quake could trigger a similar rupture near Düzce, a town roughly 60 miles east. His work persuaded authorities there to close school buildings damaged during the Izmit shaking. On November 12, a segment of the North Anatolian Fault gave way, in a magnitude 7.2. The empty school buildings collapsed.

---

[5]heretical — against the opinion of authorities

85   Lin and Stein both admit that Coulomb stress doesn't explain all
earthquakes. Indeed, some geophysicists, like Karen Felzer, of the
U.S. Geological Survey, think their hypothesis gives short shrift[6] to the
impact that dynamic stress—the actual rattling of a quake in motion—has
on neighboring faults.
90   In the aftermath of the disastrous March 11 Tōhoku quake, both camps
are looking at its well-monitored aftershocks (including several within
100 miles of Tokyo) for answers. Intriguingly, it was *preceded* by a
flurry of earthquakes, one as large as magnitude 7.2, that may have
been foreshocks, although no one thought so at the time; the researchers
95   are trying to determine what those early quakes meant.
When I ask Lin whether California, where I live, is next, he laughs.
"I understand that the public now thinks that we've entered a global
earthquake cluster. Even my own mother in China thinks that. But there's
no scientific evidence whatsoever to suggest that the earthquake in New
100 Zealand triggered the earthquake in Japan, or Japan will trigger one in
California." Still, Lin and his colleagues do wonder whether Tōhoku
has pushed neighboring faults closer to rupture. "I am particularly
interested in how this earthquake might have changed the potential of
future earthquakes to the south, even closer to Tokyo," Lin tells me.
105 "There, even a much smaller earthquake could be devastating."

—Judith Lewis Mernit
"Is San Francisco Next?"
The Atlantic, June 2011

----

[6]short shrift — little consideration

15. As used in line 6, the word "anomalies" most nearly means
(1) seasonal changes   (3) dangerous incidents
(2) odd occurrences   (4) scheduled events   15 ___

16. The first paragraph contributes to a central idea in the text by
(1) contributing historical facts   (3) comparing two philosophies
(2) contrasting early theories   (4) challenging cultural beliefs   16 ___

17. The figurative language in lines 14 and 15 conveys a sense of
(1) disbelief   (2) apathy   (3) disappointment   (4) urgency   17 ___

18. The contrast drawn between the Haicheng and Tangshan
earthquakes (lines 10 through 32) contributes to a central idea
that earthquakes are
(1) preceded by reliable signs   (3) not always predictable
(2) controlled by observable factors (4) not often studied   18 ___

19. The purpose of lines 33 through 37 is to emphasize that Jian Lin
(1) relied on his past experience to identify earthquakes
(2) modified his methods of observing earthquakes
(3) changed his understanding about the causes of earthquakes
(4) disagreed with his co-researcher on the measurement
of earthquakes   19 ___

20. The word "champions" as used in line 39 most nearly means
(1) advisers   (2) supporters   (3) adaptors   (4) survivors   20 ___

21. Which statement reflects a long-held belief disproved by Lin,
Stein, and King?
(1) "many earthquakes classified as main shocks are actually
aftershocks" (lines 43 and 44)
(2) "an earthquake that happened in one place would decrease
the possibility of another happening nearby" (lines 47 through 49)
(3) "Rocks can be subject to two kinds of stresses" (line 62)
(4) "faults in the ground behave much like rocks in the
laboratory" (lines 68 and 69)   21 ___

22. According to lines 62 through 74, seismologists realized that
the California sequence of earthquakes happened because
(1) shear stress forced rocks to fuse together
(2) clamping stress caused rocks to move apart
(3) shear stress was greater than clamping stress
(4) clamping stress balanced the shear stress   22 ___

23. Throughout the text, the author portrays Jian Lin as
(1) satisfied   (2) superstitious   (3) cautious   (4) dedicated   23 ___

24. Jian Lin's research regarding earthquakes can best be
described as
(1) flawed by inconsistent methodology
(2) concurrent with prior theories
(3) challenged by conflicting findings
(4) important to future studies   24 ___

Part 2
Argument

Directions: Closely read each of the *four* texts provided on the following pages and write a source-based argument on the topic below. You may use the margins to take notes as you read and scrap paper to plan your response. Write your argument on a separate sheet of paper provided by the teacher.

Topic: Should self-driving cars replace human drivers?

Your Task: Carefully read each of the *four* texts provided. Then, using evidence from at least *three* of the texts, write a well-developed argument regarding whether or not self-driving cars should replace human drivers. Clearly establish your claim, distinguish your claim from alternate or opposing claims, and use specific, relevant, and sufficient evidence from at least *three* of the texts to develop your argument. Do not simply summarize each text.

Guidelines:

  Be sure to:
  • Establish your claim regarding whether or not self-driving cars should replace human drivers
  • Distinguish your claim from alternate or opposing claims
  • Use specific, relevant, and sufficient evidence from at least *three* of the texts to develop your argument
  • Identify each source that you reference by text number and line number(s) or graphic (for example: Text 1, line 4 or Text 2, graphic)
  • Organize your ideas in a cohesive and coherent manner
  • Maintain a formal style of writing
  • Follow the conventions of standard written English

Texts:
  Text 1 – How Google's Self-Driving Car Will Change Everything
  Text 2 – Google's Driverless Cars Run Into Problem: Cars With Drivers
  Text 3 – Autonomous Vehicles Will Replace Taxi Drivers, But That's
           Just the Beginning
  Text 4 – Along for the Ride

Text 1
How Google's Self-Driving Car Will Change Everything

Imagine getting in your car, typing or speaking a location into your vehicle's interface, then letting it drive you to your destination while you read a book, surf the web or nap. Self-driving vehicles — the stuff of science fiction since the first roads were paved — are coming, and they're
5   going to radically change what it's like to get from point A to point B.

Basic Technology Already In Use

...The first big leap to fully autonomous[1] vehicles is due in 2017, when Google Inc. (GOOG) said it would have an integrated system ready to market. Every major automotive manufacturer is likely to follow by the early 2020s, though their systems could wind up being more sensor-
10 based, and rely less on networking and access to map information. Google probably wont [*sic*] manufacture cars. More likely, it'll license the software and systems.

A Drastic Change

As with the adoption of any new revolutionary technology, there will be problems for businesses that don't adjust fast enough. Futurists
15 estimate that hundreds of billions of dollars (if not trillions) will be lost by automakers, suppliers, dealers, insurers, parking companies, and many other car-related enterprises. And think of the lost revenue for governments via licensing fees, taxes and tolls, and by personal injury lawyers and health insurers.
20 Who needs a car made with heavier-gauge steel and eight airbags (not to mention a body shop) if accidents are so rare? Who needs a parking spot close to work if your car can drive you there, park itself miles away, only to pick you up later? Who needs to buy a flight from Boston to Cleveland when you can leave in the evening, sleep much of
25 the way, and arrive in the morning?

Indeed, Google's goal is to increase car utilization from 5-10% to 75% or more by facilitating sharing. That means fewer cars on the road. Fewer cars period, in fact. Who needs to own a car when you can just order a shared one and it'll drive up minutes later, ready to take you wherever
30 you want? ...

Changing Oil Demand

If you're in the business of finding, extracting, refining and marketing hydrocarbons,[2] such as Exxon Mobil Corp. (EOX), Chevron Corp. (CVX) or BP plc (BP), you could see your business fluctuate as use changes.

---

[1]autonomous — self–directed
[2]hydrocarbons — organic compounds that are chief components of petroleum and natural gas

"These vehicles should practice very efficient eco-driving practices,
35 which is typically about 20% better than the average driver," said
[Robin] *Chase*[3] [*sic*] "On the other hand, if these cars are owned by
individuals, I see a huge rise in the number of trips, and vehicle miles
traveled. People will send out their car to run errands they would never
do if they had to be in the car and waste their own time. If the
40 autonomous cars are shared vehicles and people pay for each trip, I think
this will reduce demand, and thus (vehicle miles traveled)."

Safety Dividend

…"Over 90% of accidents today are caused by driver error," said
Professor Robert W. Peterson of the Center for Insurance Law and
Regulation at Santa Clara University School of Law. "There is every
45 reason to believe that self-driving cars will reduce frequency and severity
of accidents, so insurance costs should fall, perhaps dramatically."

"Cars can still get flooded, damaged or stolen," notes Michael Barry,
the v.p. [vice president] of media relations at the Insurance Information
Institute. "But this technology will have a dramatic impact on under-
50 writing.[4] A lot of traditional underwriting criteria will be upended."

Barry said it's too early to quantify exactly how self-driving vehicles
will affect rates, but added that injured parties in a crash involving a
self-driving car may choose to sue the vehicle's manufacturer, or the
software company that designed the autonomous capability. …

Risks, Hurdles and the Unknown

55 There are regulatory and legislative obstacles to widespread use of
self-driving cars, and substantial concerns about privacy (who will have
access to any driving information these vehicles store?). There's also
the question of security, as hackers could theoretically take control of
these vehicles, and are not known for their restraint or civic-mindedness.

The Bottom Line

60 However it plays out, these vehicles are coming — and fast. Their full
adoption will take decades, but their convenience, cost, safety and other
factors will make them ubiquitous[5] and indispensable. Such as with any
technological revolution, the companies that plan ahead, adjust the
fastest and imagine the biggest will survive and thrive. And companies
65 invested in old technology and practices will need to evolve or risk dying.

—Joseph A. Dallegro
excerpted and adapted from
"How Google's Self-Driving Car Will Change Everything"
www.investopedia.com, 2015

---

[3]Robin Chase — founder and CEO of Buzzcar
[4]underwriting — risk determination
[5]ubiquitous — everywhere

Text 2
Google's Driverless Cars Run Into Problem: Cars With Drivers

Google, a leader in efforts to create driverless cars, has run into an odd safety conundrum:[1] humans.

Last month, as one of Google's self-driving cars approached a cross-walk, it did what it was supposed to do when it slowed to allow a
5   pedestrian to cross, prompting its "safety driver" to apply the brakes. The pedestrian was fine, but not so much Google's car, which was hit from behind by a human-driven sedan.

Google's fleet of autonomous test cars is programmed to follow the letter of the law. But it can be tough to get around if you are a stickler for
10   the rules. One Google car, in a test in 2009, couldn't get through a four-way stop because its sensors kept waiting for other (human) drivers to stop completely and let it go. The human drivers kept inching forward, looking for the advantage — paralyzing Google's robot.

It is not just a Google issue. Researchers in the fledgling[2] field of
15   autonomous vehicles say that one of the biggest challenges facing automated cars is blending them into a world in which humans don't behave by the book. "The real problem is that the car is too safe," said Donald Norman, director of the Design Lab at the University of California, San Diego, who studies autonomous vehicles. ...
20   Traffic wrecks and deaths could well plummet in a world without any drivers, as some researchers predict. But wide use of self-driving cars is still many years away, and testers are still sorting out hypothetical risks — like hackers — and real world challenges, like what happens when an autonomous car breaks down on the highway.
25   For now, there is the nearer-term problem of blending robots and humans. Already, cars from several automakers have technology that can warn or even take over for a driver, whether through advanced cruise control or brakes that apply themselves. Uber is working on the self-driving car technology, and Google expanded its tests in July to
30   Austin, Tex[as].

Google cars regularly take quick, evasive maneuvers or exercise caution in ways that are at once the most cautious approach, but also out of step with the other vehicles on the road. ...

Since 2009, Google cars have been in 16 crashes, mostly fender-
35   benders, and in every single case, the company says, a human was at fault. This includes the rear-ender crash on Aug. 20, and reported Tuesday by Google. The Google car slowed for a pedestrian, then the Google employee manually applied the brakes. The car was hit from behind, sending the employee to the emergency room for mild whiplash.

---

[1]conundrum — difficult problem
[2]fledgling — new and inexperienced

40   Google's report on the incident adds another twist: While the safety driver did the right thing by applying the brakes, if the autonomous car had been left alone, it might have braked less hard and traveled closer to the crosswalk, giving the car behind a little more room to stop. Would that have prevented the collision? Google says it's impossible to say.

45   There was a single case in which Google says the company was responsible for a crash. It happened in August 2011, when one of its Google cars collided with another moving vehicle. But, remarkably, the Google car was being piloted at the time by an employee. Another human at fault. ...

50   On a recent outing with New York Times journalists, the Google driverless car took two evasive maneuvers that simultaneously displayed how the car errs on the cautious side, but also how jarring that experience can be. In one maneuver, it swerved sharply in a residential neighborhood to avoid a car that was poorly parked, so much so that the Google sensors

55   couldn't tell if it might pull into traffic.

More jarring for human passengers was a maneuver that the Google car took as it approached a red light in moderate traffic. The laser system mounted on top of the driverless car sensed that a vehicle coming the other direction was approaching the red light at higher-than-safe speeds.

60   The Google car immediately jerked to the right in case it had to avoid a collision. In the end, the oncoming car was just doing what human drivers so often do: not approach a red light cautiously enough, though the driver did stop well in time.

Courtney Hohne, a spokeswoman for the Google project, said current

65   testing was devoted to "smoothing out" the relationship between the car's software and humans. For instance, at four-way stops, the program lets the car inch forward, as the rest of us might, asserting its turn while looking for signs that it is being allowed to go.

The way humans often deal with these situations is that "they make

70   eye contact. On the fly, they make agreements about who has the right of way," said John Lee, a professor of industrial and systems engineering and expert in driver safety and automation at the University of Wisconsin.

"Where are the eyes in an autonomous vehicle?" he added. ...

—Matt Richtel and Conor Dougherty
excerpted and adapted from
"Google's Driverless Cars Run Into Problem: Cars With Drivers"
www.nytimes.com, Sept. 1, 2015

Text 3
Autonomous Vehicles Will Replace Taxi Drivers,
But That's Just the Beginning

...According to the Bureau of Labor Statistics [BLS] there are about 178,000 people employed as taxi drivers or chauffeurs in the United States. But once driverless technology advances to the point that vehicles can be fully autonomous — without the need for any human behind
5 the wheel in case of emergencies — professional drivers will become a thing of the past. Bus drivers, whether they're for schools, cities, or long-distance travel, would be made obsolete. Once cars drive themselves, food deliveries will be a matter of restaurants filling a car with orders and sending it off, eliminating the need for a delivery driver. Each of
10 these professions employ more people and are better paid than taxi drivers, as shown in the table below.

Occupation	Average annual wage	Number of jobs	Total annual wages
Taxi drivers & chauffeurs	$25,690	178,260	$4,579,499,400
Bus drivers – transit & intercity	$39,410	158,050	$6,228,750,500
Driver / sales workers (delivering food, newspapers)	$27,720	405,810	$11,249,053,200
Bus drivers – school or special client	$29,910	499,440	$14,938,250,400
Postal service mail carriers	$51,790	307,490	$15,924,907,100
Light truck or delivery services drivers (UPS, FedEx)	$33,870	797,010	$26,994,728,700
Heavy and tractor-trailer truck drivers	$41,930	1,625,290	$68,148,409,700
TOTAL	$35,760.00	3,971,350	$148,063,599,000.00

Source: Bureau of Labor Statistics

Some of these may be a bit surprising, like postal carriers. But once fully autonomous vehicles are commonplace it would make sense for the Postal Service to make use of the technology to deliver mail, especially
15 in areas where curbside mailboxes are standard and it would be rather simple for a mechanical arm to deposit and retrieve mail directly. Drivers of delivery trucks for companies like UPS and FedEx may also face extinction, if they're not replaced by Amazon's delivery drones first — or perhaps they'll develop a combined system where self-driving
20 trucks bring packages from the warehouse to their destination, and a drone delivers them the last few yards from curbside to doorstep.

Despite their importance for the economy, each of these professions pale [*sic*] in comparison to heavy and tractor-trailer truck drivers. This field employs the most by far — nine times as many people work as
25   truckers than as taxi drivers, and it's the most common job in a whopping 29 states — and is also better paid than most, with an average salary of about $42,000. When considering the total amount of wages paid to each of the seven occupations in the table above, truck drivers make up nearly half, while taxi drivers & chauffeurs only account for 3%.
30   The development of self-driving tractor-trailers won't be far behind automated taxi cabs, with companies like Daimler already testing out partially-automated trucks in Nevada.

While there may be other driving-focused jobs not included in these BLS statistics, there are certainly many more industries that will be
35   impacted by the replacement of humans with self-driving vehicles. If this technology leads to a sharp decline in car ownership like many predict, insurance companies will have far fewer customers and may not need as many employees to service them. The same goes for mechanics and auto part manufacturers, who could face a massive drop in demand.
40   Fewer human truckers on the road means fewer motel stays and rest stop visits, and cheaper trucking could take business away from freight trains or even oil pipelines. Vehicles programmed to obey traffic laws won't need nearly as much policing, which also means fewer traffic tickets and less revenue for municipalities. The full scale of these economic
45   shifts will be impossible to understand until they're upon us, but the one thing we can know for sure is that they'll touch almost every aspect of society. ...

—Sam Tracy
excerpted and adapted from "Autonomous Vehicles Will
Replace Taxi Drivers, But That's Just the Beginning"
www.huffingtonpost.com, June 11, 2015

Text 4
Along for the Ride

...Automotive designers have a good incentive to get human drivers out from behind the wheel: public safety. In 2012, according to the most recent figures from the National Highway Traffic Safety Administration (NHTSA), 33,561 people were killed in car crashes in the United States,
5   and an estimated 2.36 million were injured. According to NHTSA, a number of major crash studies have found that human error caused more than 90 percent of those crashes. In a perfect world, technology would take driver error out of the equation. ...

But before society can reap those benefits, experts caution there are
10   important problems to solve. Namely, since people interact with technology in unexpected ways, how will each individual driver engage with an automated car?

For some people, automation might lead to complacency,[1] says Nicholas Ward, PhD, a human factors psychologist in the department of

15 mechanical and industrial engineering at Montana State University. Drivers who put too much trust in automation may become overly reliant on it, overestimating what the system can do for them. ...

Information overload may be another concern, says Neville Stanton, PhD, a psychologist at the University of Southampton in the United
20 Kingdom, who studies human performance in technological systems. While automated systems are designed to take pressures off the driver, he's found that they may add complexity in some cases. In an automated system, drivers may feel compelled to monitor the behavior of the system as well as keep an eye on the driving environment. That extra pressure
25 might increase stress and error. ...

Given a nearly infinite combination of driver personalities, road conditions and vehicle technologies, the answer is anything but straight-forward. In a study using a driving simulator, for example, Stanton found that adaptive cruise control — in which a car maintains a safe
30 following distance from the vehicle ahead of it — can reduce a driver's mental workload and stress levels. However, that technology also caused a reduction in drivers' situational awareness. And while a lower mental workload may be a good thing in tricky traffic jams, it could cause problems if drivers totally tune out.
35   Indeed, driver disengagement is a serious concern for automated-car designers. Users in such vehicles are expected to tune out. After all, the appeal of such cars is that they can transport us to and fro without our having to do the hard work. But that presents a problem for our busy brains. ...
40   Detached from the activity of driving, most people soon begin to experience "passive fatigue," says Gerald Matthews, PhD, a psychologist at the Applied Cognition and Training in Immersive Virtual Environments Lab at the University of Central Florida. That cognitive muddling can be a big problem, Matthews says, if the driver has to take
45 back control of the vehicle (when leaving a highway "platoon" of automated cars to re-enter city streets, for instance — or, in a worst-case scenario, if automated systems fail). ...

Like it or not, though, carmakers are pressing forward with automated systems, and psychologists can play a role in making them as safe as
50 possible. One important issue, says Pradhan,[2] is how drivers of different ages, personalities, experience levels and cognitive abilities will deal with such systems. "There is no average driver. The field is so new, we're still asking a lot of fundamental questions — and there are very few people looking at driver characteristics," he says. "Automation has to be
55 designed for everybody." ...

—Kirsten Weir

excerpted from "Along for the Ride" www.apa.org, January 2015

---

[1]complacency — a feeling of security, often while unaware of potential dangers
[2]Anuj K. Pradhan, PhD — a research scientist who studies driver behavior and injury prevention at the University of Michigan Transportation Research Institute

Part 3
Text-Analysis Response

Your Task: Closely read the text provided on the following pages and write a well-developed, text-based response of two to three paragraphs. In your response, identify a central idea in the text and analyze how the author's use of *one* writing strategy (literary element or literary technique or rhetorical device) develops this central idea. Use strong and thorough evidence from the text to support your analysis. Do *not* simply summarize the text. You may use the margins to take notes as you read and scrap paper to plan your response. Write your response on a separate sheet of paper.

Guidelines:

Be sure to:
- Identify a central idea in the text
- Analyze how the author's use of *one* writing strategy (literary element or literary technique or rhetorical device) develops this central idea. Examples include: characterization, conflict, denotation/connotation, metaphor, simile, irony, language use, point-of-view, setting, structure, symbolism, theme, tone, etc.
- Use strong and thorough evidence from the text to support your analysis
- Organize your ideas in a cohesive and coherent manner
- Maintain a formal style of writing
- Follow the conventions of standard written English

Text

The following excerpt is taken from a novel set in France during the World War II era.

  Sixteen paces to the water fountain, sixteen back. Forty-two to the stairwell, forty-two back. Marie-Laure draws maps in her head, unreels a hundred yards of imaginary twine, and then turns and reels it back in. Botany smells like glue and blotter paper and pressed flowers. Paleontology
5 smells like rock dust, bone dust. Biology smells like formalin and old fruit; it is loaded with heavy cool jars in which float things she has only had described for her: the pale coiled ropes of rattlesnakes, the severed hands of gorillas. Entomology smells like mothballs and oil: a preservative that, Dr. Geffard explains, is called naphthalene. Offices smell of carbon paper,
10 or cigar smoke, or brandy, or perfume. Or all four.

  She follows cables and pipes, railings and ropes, hedges and sidewalks. She startles people. She never knows if the lights are on.

  The children she meets brim with questions: Does it hurt? Do you shut your eyes to sleep? How do you know what time it is?
15 It doesn't hurt, she explains. And there is no darkness, not the kind they imagine. Everything is composed of webs and lattices and upheavals of sound and texture. She walks a circle around the Grand Gallery, navigating between squeaking floorboards; she hears feet tramp up and down museum staircases, a toddler squeal, the groan of a weary grandmother

20   lowering herself onto a bench.
          Color—that's another thing people don't expect. In her imagination,
      in her dreams, everything has color. The museum buildings are beige,
      chestnut, hazel. Its scientists are lilac and lemon yellow and fox brown.
      Piano chords loll in the speaker of the wireless in the guard station,
25   projecting rich blacks and complicated blues down the hall toward the key
      pound.[1] Church bells send arcs of bronze careening off the windows. Bees
      are silver; pigeons are ginger and auburn and occasionally golden. The huge
      cypress trees she and her father pass on their morning walk are shimmering
      kaleidoscopes, each needle a polygon of light.
30   She has no memories of her mother but imagines her as white, a
      soundless brilliance. Her father radiates a thousand colors, opal, strawberry
      red, deep russet, wild green; a smell like oil and metal, the feel of a
      lock tumbler sliding home, the sound of his key rings chiming as he walks.
      He is an olive green when he talks to a department head, an escalating series
35   of oranges when he speaks to Mademoiselle Fleury from the greenhouses,
      a bright red when he tries to cook. He glows sapphire when he sits over
      his workbench in the evenings, humming almost inaudibly as he works,
      the tip of his cigarette gleaming a prismatic blue.
          She gets lost. Secretaries or botanists, and once the director's assistant,
40   bring her back to the key pound. She is curious; she wants to know the
      difference between an alga and a lichen, a *Diplodon charruanus* and a
      Diplodon delodontus. Famous men take her by the elbow and escort her
      through the gardens or guide her up stairwells. "I have a daughter too,"
      they'll say. Or "I found her among the hummingbirds."
45   "*Toutes mes excuses*,"[2] her father says. He lights a cigarette; he plucks
      key after key out of her pockets. "What," he whispers, "am I going to do
      with you?"
          On her ninth birthday, when she wakes, she finds two gifts. The first is
      a wooden box with no opening she can detect. She turns it this way and
50   that. It takes her a little while to realize one side is spring-loaded; she
      presses it and the box flips open. Inside waits a single cube of creamy
      Camembert that she pops directly into in [*sic*] her mouth.
          "Too easy!" her father says, laughing.
          The second gift is heavy, wrapped in paper and twine. Inside is a massive
55   spiral-bound book. In Braille.
          "They said it's for boys. Or very adventurous girls." She can hear him
      smiling.
          She slides her fingertips across the embossed[3] title page. *Around. The.*
      World. In. Eighty. Days. "Papa, it's too expensive."
60   "That's for me to worry about."

---

[1]key pound — the office of her father, the museum locksmith
[2]*toutes mes excuses* — my apologies
[3]embossed — a stamped, molded or carved design

That morning Marie-Laure crawls beneath the counter of the key pound and lies on her stomach and sets all ten fingertips in a line on a page. The French feels old-fashioned, the dots printed much closer together than she is used to. But after a week, it becomes easy. She finds the ribbon she uses
65   as a bookmark, opens the book, and the museum falls away.

Mysterious Mr. Fogg lives his life like a machine. Jean Passepartout becomes his obedient valet. When, after two months, she reaches the novel's last line, she flips back to the first page and starts again. At night she runs her fingertips over her father's model: the bell tower, the display windows.
70   She imagines Jules Verne's characters walking along the streets, chatting in shops; a half-inch-tall baker slides speck-sized loaves in and out of his ovens; three minuscule burglars hatch plans as they drive slowly past the jeweler's; little grumbling cars throng the rue[4] de Mirbel, wipers sliding back and forth. Behind a fourth-floor window on the rue des Patriarches,
75   a miniature version of her father sits at a miniature workbench in their miniature apartment, just as he does in real life, sanding away at some infinitesimal[5]piece of wood; across the room is a miniature girl, skinny, quick-witted,an open book in her lap; inside her chest pulses something huge, something full of longing, something unafraid.

—Anthony Doerr
excerpted from *All the Light We Cannot See*, 2014
Scribner

---

[4]rue — street
[5]infinitesimal — very small